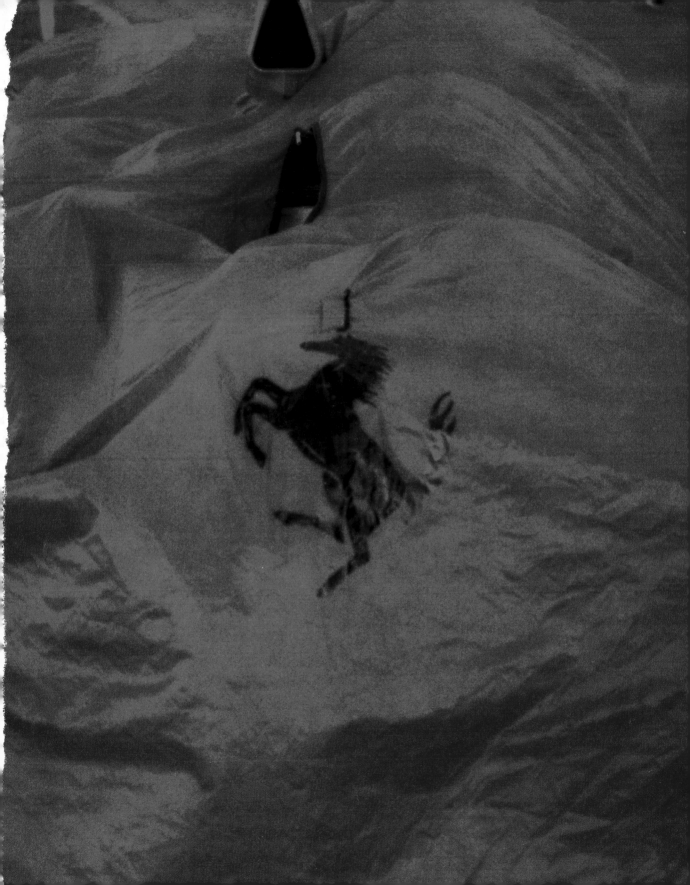

Formula Ferrari

THE FIRST OFFICIAL INSIDE STORY
OF THE MOST SUCCESSFUL TEAM
IN THE HISTORY OF FORMULA 1

Umberto Zapelloni
Photography by Michel Comte

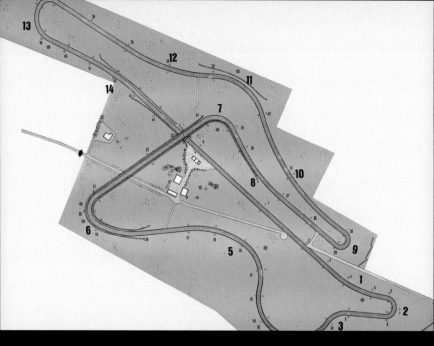

First Published in Great Britain in 2004 by Hodder & Stoughton
a division of Hodder Headline Ltd

Copyright © 2004 Scuderia Ferrari
Text copyright © 2004 Umberto Zapelloni
Photographs copyright © 2004 Lucas Albers and Ivan Colombo

10 9 8 7 6 5 4 3 2 1

CONTENTS

CONSTRUCTORS' WORLD CHAMPIONSHIP TROPHY, 2003

INTRODUCTION

Formula Ferrari is the story of a dream that has become reality, the tale of how a team rewrote the record book and assumed a unique position in the world of Formula 1.

Ferrari were already assured of a place in the annals of the sport's history by virtue of being the only team to have competed in every year of the Formula 1 world championship. However, the current incarnation of the team, which has won every drivers' title this century, has attained legendary status not just in Formula 1 but in the sporting arena as a whole. The records and victories will stand forever, testament to a fairytale come true. Fathers will tell it to their children, grandparents to their grandchildren and so on down the years. The team and the company have come to represent a benchmark in both sporting and industrial terms and their achievements have given the whole of Italy a cause for pride.

Luca di Montezemolo, Michael Schumacher, Jean Todt, Ross Brawn, Rory Byrne and Paolo Martinelli are the chief architects of this colossus. Backing them up, starting with Rubens Barrichello and Luca Badoer, are a further eight hundred people, all of whom have contributed to what for so long looked impossible — becoming and continuing to be the best, winning five constructors' and four drivers' titles in a row in the process. From Schumacher to the office cleaner, everyone is committed to making the team virtually invincible. Work and passion bind them together. That is Formula Ferrari.

Umberto Zapelloni

*THE ITALIAN GRAND PRIX
2003 (MONZA)*

*THE JAPANESE GRAND PRIX
2003 (SUZUKA)*

*THE SAN MARINO GRAND
PRIX 2003 (IMOLA)*

*THE US GRAND PRIX 2003
(INDIANAPOLIS)*

1

A DROP OF WATER IN THE DESERT

Ferrari start again from scratch

On an autumn's day in 1991 — 15 November to be precise — Ferrari issued a press release announcing the appointment of a new president, Luca di Montezemolo. The prodigal son had returned. Montezemolo had been sporting director in the mid-seventies, during Niki Lauda's glory days, and since then his experiences with Italy's America's Cup syndicate, and with the Italia '90 football World Cup and Juventus, had groomed him for the far more difficult challenge that he was about to undertake. He would no longer be 'Ingegner' Ferrari's right-hand man — he was going to replace him. 'President and managing director' said the press release and that meant Luca di Montezemolo would have total control over the running of not only the Formula 1 team, but also, more importantly, the entire company.

Ferrari were a team in crisis, despite having taken second place in the 1990 world championship. Alain Prost failed to win the title because of a vendetta with Ayrton Senna. The Brazilian forced him off the track at the first corner at Suzuka in the penultimate race of the season. This was the era of McLaren-Honda and Williams-Renault and the fierce struggles between Senna, Prost and Nigel Mansell. Ferrari made the headlines for sackings, failures and in-house fighting.

Cesare Fiorio, who had won everything with Lancia in rallying, had been brought to Maranello in something of a panic in 1989, charged with rebuilding the team and restoring it to a position worthy of its status. But results were not forthcoming, and the factory was having little success in terms of sales. Before the 1991 season began, Fiorio was sacked.

Prost, disillusioned, had already left, voicing his opinion that 'a truck would be easier to drive than this car'. In the space of a few months, the Ferrari that had been a contender had all but vanished. Montezemolo recalls having to deal with mechanics who took themselves for Ron Dennis and with engineers who, after a few months, declared that they were incapable of designing the car of the future. The team had no motivation and lacked the strength even to consider staging a resurrection.

At first, Montezemolo called on old friends, taking on Niki Lauda as a consultant and employing Sante Ghedini, who had been manager in the Lauda days. Jean Alesi and Ivan Capelli had already been signed as drivers, and engineer Claudio Lombardi had been handed the team management role. However, it did not take the new president long to realise that a radical reorganisation was required. When he convened a meeting with those in charge of the project to build the new car with which to defend Ferrari's colours in 1992, too many people knocked on his office door. Too many people were getting their hands on the car. To get Ferrari to the point of breaking records, and winning left, right and centre, was going to involve a lot of hard work by motivated staff, and there were likely to be a few 'transitional years'. New cars were needed on the track and on the streets, where the 348 and the Testarossa were obsolete models. Amalgamating all the necessary ingredients was not going to be the work of a moment — the first task was to find those ingredients — but in Formula 1, time is in short supply.

Montezemolo took the reins of Ferrari one hundred days before the first race of the 1992 season, for which the team had to use the famous 'double flat bottom' car, a beast that was a real handful. Alesi managed to get it to the podium twice, while the hapless Capelli never made it and was sacked before the end of the season. The twenty-one points scored during that season summarise the difficulty of the situation. A new way had to be found and new men had to be entrusted with the job.

The next date that needs to be underlined in red is 1 July 1993, the day Jean Todt started work for Ferrari. The man who masterminded Peugeot's success in rallying, rally-raid and sports prototypes was put in charge of a team that had not tasted victory since the Spanish Grand Prix on 30 September 1990. Partnering Alesi by this time was Austrian Gerhard Berger, another Prancing Horse returnee. He had been put forward by Niki Lauda because Lauda felt Berger could bring valuable experience from his three years spent alongside Senna at McLaren.

But good results were still a long way off. The French Grand Prix — the first with Todt at the helm — exemplified what he was up against. Alesi retired with a broken engine and Berger finished fourteenth, two laps down on the winner, Alain Prost in the Williams-Renault. The Italian media were sceptical about Todt's chances of success, making his task even more difficult, although none other than the respected Bernie Ecclestone was in favour of his appointment. 'Mr. E', as he is known to insiders, forged the modern incarnation of Formula 1, turning the sport into big business, and in fact, he was the one who suggested Todt's name to Montezemolo. Ferrari are the only team to have competed in the world championship since its inception, the only team with fans scattered around the world, so it was natural that the team's well being should be important to the sport's ringmaster. Montezemolo did not waste any time. He did his research, asked the opinion of others and then, as usual, took his own decision.

The first meeting between Todt and the Ferrari president took place in the summer of 1992. Todt nearly blew it there and then, turning up at the wheel of a Mercedes. Matteo, the president's son, still laughs when he recalls his father's face as Monsieur Todt stepped out of the car. But Jean Todt has always relished a challenge. He had won all there was to win in rallying, desert raids and the Le Mans 24 Hours. Therefore Formula 1 represented the highest and final challenge. 'I chose him because the entire team needed a complete shake-up,' Montezemolo recalls. Methodically and with a huge amount of work, Jean Todt laid the foundations for a reconstruction that has lasted to this day.

The early days were complicated for him. From the summer of 1992, the car's design had been entrusted to John Barnard, which, as it turned out, was the wrong plan of action. Barnard worked out of

England in what was effectively Ferrari's technology satellite, but he worked at his own pace. His designs were refined but complex and always arrived at Maranello at the last minute. The people who came up with the ideas in England and those who turned them into metal at Maranello never reached the level of understanding required to hit the target. On top of that, the chassis and engine specialists worked completely independently of one another.

The only positive aspect of this arrangement was the fact that many young engineers were able to experience life in the heart of Formula 1's Silicon Valley in England, and from among these came the group who formed a key element in the creation of a new Ferrari. One such is former naval officer Luca Baldisserri, who went on to be race engineer for Berger, Irvine and Schumacher.

'I came to Ferrari after obtaining a degree in electrical engineering from the University of Bologna, and back in '89, I joined John Barnard, who was working on the new steering-wheel-mounted gear change, which revolutionised Formula 1. He was the first to twig that electronics could be applied to all components of the car and not just to the engine. Then, when John was contracted to Ferrari again in '92, I went to England. It was a very useful experience, even if John was a complex person. I learnt the discipline of English work methods and how to tackle problems step by step. It all helped when the role of electronics in Formula 1 was reduced and I started to work as a race engineer with the drivers.'

The experiment with John Barnard and his technology centre served to point the team down the right road. 'The first drops of rain will begin to fall in the desert,' commented Montezemolo after a rare podium finish for Alesi in 1992. When he came second in the 1993 Italian Grand Prix at Monza, at a time when just getting to the chequered flag was an achievement, it really did seem to have the same importance as a glass of water to a lone and thirsty traveller walking in the desert.

In 1992, Ferrari picked up twenty-one world championship points and the following year, twenty-eight. This was a low point and a far cry from earlier years. Ferrari's first victory came on 14 July 1951 in the British Grand Prix, and world titles followed in 1952 and 1953 courtesy of Alberto Ascari, then in 1956 with Juan Manuel Fangio, 1958 with Mike Hawthorn and 1961 with the American, Phil Hill. Championship winning resumed in 1975 and 1977 with Lauda — Montezemolo was sporting director for Niki's first title. This series ended in 1979 with Jody Scheckter and after that, nothing. There were the dreams of Gilles Villeneuve and the great sadness that followed his death. Didier Pironi provided emotion, Patrick Tambay an illusion, while Mansell and Prost shone, but there were no world championship titles. It seemed to be a curse. Ten years went by, then twenty, and the titles always went elsewhere.

The long road back, at least in terms of winning races, began on 31 July 1994, with Gerhard Berger at the German Grand Prix. After 1400 days and fifty-eight grands prix without a win, Ferrari were back on the top step once again and on that July day Michael Schumacher, who was heading for his first championship title, began to mull over the idea of going to work in a red race suit. The explosion of enthusiasm from the Ferrari fans, most of whom probably drove Mercedes or BMWs, impressed Schumacher. The sight of their Prancing Horse flags fluttering in the breeze at a German circuit as they cheered home an Austrian driver maybe convinced him that driving and winning for Ferrari would have been really something unique. Thus, a year later, having taken his second title with Benetton, Schumacher was unable to resist the overtures of Luca di Montezemolo and Jean Todt.

So 16 August 1995 is the third date in the Ferrari history book to be underlined in red. The announcement stated that Michael Schumacher would drive a Maranello car from the start of 1996. Ferrari had opted for the number one, the reigning world champion, a driver with a winning past and, more importantly, a winning future ahead of him. As far as Montezemolo and Todt were concerned, they had a clear plan mapped out not only to become winners again, but also to build for the future.

The first time Montezemolo and Todt spoke about the possibility of employing Schumacher was in the spring of 1995. In one of the little notebooks that Todt uses to jot down his thoughts and job lists was written 'driver problems for 1996'. Neither the president nor Todt had any doubts that Schumacher was the best man available and Ferrari had to go for him.

So now Maranello had a world champion under its aegis once again. Apparently, Ferrari had been interested in two other world champions before then and both Senna and Prost might have ended up at Ferrari.

'I met Senna at the Villa d'Este hotel just before the 1993 Italian Grand Prix,' Todt revealed, prior to the 2004 season. 'By then, Ayrton had already decided to leave McLaren, but at the time, we were not in a position to give him a truly competitive car. In the end, fate stepped in to prevent our discussions going any further.'

Also in 1993, Prost took his fourth world title and decided to retire at the top. Two years later, at a time when Ferrari was in negotiation with Schumacher, Alain got in touch with Todt to sound out the chances of coming back to Maranello after the messy divorce of 1991. Todt listened because he wanted to have an option up his sleeve in case the dialogue with the Benetton driver came to nothing.

For 1996, Alesi and Berger were still in the frame, but a step up the ladder meant they had to aim high. It was decided that Alesi, who had given so much to Ferrari and got so much out of it, would have to go, especially as he no longer enjoyed an easy relationship with Todt. Berger could have stayed on, but he decided he did not want to partner Schumacher, having worked alongside Senna for three years. In the end, the Ferrari duo moved as one to Flavio Briatore's Benetton team. The results are there in the record books — Ferrari began winning again while Benetton began losing.

SCHUMI

*TESTING AT BARCELONA
PRE-SEASON, 1998*

2

MEN OF GOLD

The union of Montezemolo, Todt and Schumacher heralds a new era. Rory Byrne and Ross Brawn join Paolo Martinelli and the 'dream team' is born.

In 1995, it fell to Jean Todt to sound out the possibilities of the reigning world champion joining Ferrari. Schumacher was in the running to take a second consecutive title with Benetton, which meant he could bring the coveted number 1 with him to Maranello, but this was not the reason behind Ferrari chasing after him. Montezemolo and Todt were convinced that in order to keep Ferrari moving forward, they had to go for the only driver who could make the difference on the track.

The first meetings with Schumacher's manager, Willy Weber, the famous 'Mr 20 per cent', took place at Nice airport and Todt realised immediately that a deal was on the cards and not just because of the financial package on offer. Schumacher had not satiated his thirst for winning, or his taste for a challenge, and wanted to move his career forward.

August was the month for weddings. On the 5th, Michael married Corinna and on the 16th he tied the knot with Ferrari. His life was about to change and he soon realised the enormity of what was about to happen when he met Montezemolo and Todt on board Gianni Agnelli's yacht, off the coast of Monaco.

On the Thursday prior to the Hungarian Grand Prix, Agnelli spilt the beans about Schumacher's imminent signing. It had been rumoured in three Italian daily papers but the Fiat patriarch pre-empted any official announcement when he let slip the news to journalists in Villar Perosa, scene of the traditional pre-season football match between the two Juventus squads. Official denials were the order of the day in Budapest, but they fooled no one and a few days later the agreement was confirmed.

With Schumacher on board, Luca di Montezemolo and Jean Todt could set about creating a team that would triumph by the end of the nineties. The strongest team in the history of Formula 1 was on the up and up.

Paolo Martinelli was already ensconced at the head of the engine department. He had been with the company since leaving Bologna University with an engineering degree in 1978. Born in Modena on 29 September 1952, as a schoolboy his bedroom walls were decorated with pictures of Niki Lauda's Ferrari, and when he walked through the gates at Maranello, he was realising his childhood dream. Martinelli was first assigned to the GT department, designing engines for the road-going cars. His intuitive feel for the job made him stand out from his peers, and he caught the eye of his boss, Amedeo Felisa. Montezemolo reckoned Martinelli was the right man for the team, Todt recruited him and from January 1995, Martinelli was put in charge of Ferrari's Formula 1 engine project, tasked with looking for power, reliability and ease of use.

This department has always been held in special regard by Ferrari and now Martinelli has around a hundred staff, plus another thirty who look after engines for the Sauber team. The majority of the employees are Italian, thanks to the exceptional relationship that links Ferrari to the local universities, but there are also several German and French engineers, such as the head of the engine design office, Gilles Simon, known for their expertise in the fields of metallurgy and aerospace engineering.

One man who has witnessed first hand Ferrari's rise over the past few years is Stefano Domenicali, the current team manager. He joined Ferrari fresh from Bologna University with a business and economics degree, having also been the youngest ever race director in the motorcycle world championship. Born in Imola and educated in Bologna, Domenicali is a great example of the way the Prancing Horse feeds off local talent.

'At the start,' he says, 'I looked after the budget and then moved to human resources. It was in this role that I watched the transformation of the team. I moved to the Gestione Sportiva [the racing department] at the same time as Todt arrived in July of '93 and I looked after all the hirings during this time, when the team was divided into two parts, one in England and the other in Italy. It was a time when everyone seemed to look after his own interests and there was not much team spirit. New people joined, but even the old hands understood the need for change and little by little the team took shape around Todt, who did a great job of immediately grasping where and when he needed to intervene and where things were not operating at their best.'

In 1997, Domenicali became team manager, one of the key players and the acknowledged expert when it comes to knowing the sport's rulebook. With a seat on the pit wall, on two occasions, Suzuka in 2001 and Hockenheim in 2002, he has had the honour of stepping up to the podium to pick up the constructors' trophy. Today, he is one of the people in closest contact with the drivers.

'Luckily, I am almost the same age as Schumacher and our relationship goes much deeper than just working together. Over the years, Michael has changed a lot. In the beginning, he exuded pure professionalism only, but now he has opened up and displays a more human side. He is very different from the image he projects. I have seen him do things to help others that you would not believe. And he does it without wanting anyone to find out.'

Michael Schumacher joined a Ferrari team that had won just two races in five years — Gerhard Berger won the 1994 German Grand Prix, and Jean Alesi won the Canadian in 1995. He left a team with which he had just won two world titles to take up a job that had proved too much for drivers of the calibre of Nigel Mansell and Alain Prost. The challenge would have appealed to Ayrton Senna, the greatest of them all, who died on 1 May 1994.

When Schumacher met the media at Maranello on 15 November 1995, he insisted that nobody should expect miracles. In 1996 there would be wins, and by 1997 the team would be in the running for the championship. The promises were kept, even though he did not have an easy start to his career in red. In Australia, he was tripped up by a brake problem on lap thirty-four and it took seven races for him to win. At the Nurburgring, he came home glued to the back of the Williams driven by Jacques Villeneuve, son of Gilles, celebrating his first Formula 1 win. At Imola, he picked up his first pole position as a Ferrarista and another second place, sixteen seconds behind another son of a famous father — Damon Hill in a Williams-Renault. He took a second pole in Monaco, but on the opening lap, between the Loews and Portier corners, he crashed into the guard rail. A first win continued to elude him, but the scent of victory was in the air.

It came in the Spanish Grand Prix, 2 June 1996. Rain hardly does justice to the conditions. It was a deluge. The track looked like a river in full flow and Schumacher drove his Ferrari F310 as though it was a powerboat.

The upward trend, started in the days of Berger and Alesi, was now plain for all to see. Ferrari was once again competitive at the highest level and in the running for top honours in the constructors' category. At the same time, the rest of the team had immediately realised what sort of person they were dealing with in Michael Schumacher. His qualities emerged as soon as pre-season testing began at Estoril in Portugal. Michael did his first test with the team there in 1995, at the wheel of a 412T.

'We were due to do a test session,' some of the lads in the garage recall. 'We turned up at 8.15 as usual. He was already there in his race suit, sitting on the steps of the motorhome. He looked at us and smiled, saying, "If you want to start winning, you have to get up early in the morning." That was our first meeting.'

Luca Baldisserri was Schumi's race engineer for the first three of his title-winning seasons with Ferrari. 'I started working with Michael after looking after Eddie Irvine,' he says. 'It was not straightforward for me because you need to develop a good understanding between engineer and driver as quickly as possible. Eddie was very intuitive when it came to set-up, but not very diligent in watching every detail. Michael is also extraordinarily sensitive and whatever the car is doing he will deliver one hundred per cent. If the car has a problem, Michael adapts his driving style to get round it, so that you hardly notice it as he gets the most out of the car. It is something that did not happen with Eddie, nor does it with Rubens [Barrichello]. It is a gift and helps get results, but it can hide problems with the car, making it seem perfect when it is not. It is in this area that one can see just how extraordinary he is. However, Michael will still accept guidance in certain areas, especially when it comes to tyres, which is a tough subject to master. He is quick to thank those who work with him and many times after a race, he has made a point of thanking those who have helped him make the right choices.'

The win in Barcelona was the first for a Ferrari 10 cylinder engine, the 046, fitted to the last car designed by John Barnard. The 046 was the first V10 engine designed and built at Maranello. Over the past fifty years, Ferrari had raced and won with 4, 6, 8 and twelve cylinder engines.

'When I joined the Gestione Sportiva, work on the ten cylinder had only just begun,' recalls Martinelli. 'An engine is not designed because it is the nicest or the most powerful, but because it is best suited to the total package. The aim is to produce a car that is quick, reliable and easy to drive. The ten cylinder fitted the bill. Of course, our experience with the 3,500cc twelve cylinder was a great help, as the individual cylinder size is very similar to a 3,000cc ten cylinder — 300cc is a perfect size in combustion terms.'

Schumacher's team-mate when he started with Ferrari was Eddie Irvine, who came from Jordan where he had been paired with Rubens Barrichello. In character, he is diametrically opposed to Schumacher and that is probably why they got on so well for such a long time. They formed one of the most enduring partnerships in Ferrari's history. Schumacher's first year with the team produced three wins, second place in the constructors' championship and third in the drivers' classification. It was a notable step forward.

In between the win in Spain, at the beginning of June, and victory in Belgium, at the end of August, races were marked by retirements and failures. Schumacher never pointed the finger at the team, never questioned his decision, never went back on his claim to prefer the challenge of racing for Ferrari rather than opting for the easier choices that might have been on the cards with Williams. He thus strengthened the team's resolve when it came to fending off criticism. On occasions, he never even got off the line, and other times the car let him down when he was in the lead, but he always sided with Ferrari and the team. Montezemolo and Todt certainly appreciated his loyalty, and in the end, first at Spa and then at Monza, they were rewarded with two wins that made the season even sweeter.

This was especially the case at Monza, in the Italian Grand Prix, which Ferrari had not won since 1988, where the delight of around a hundred thousand tifosi, dressed from top to toe in red, made up for all the bitter moments. Schumacher was so happy that he let the whole world know he was soon to become a father (his daughter was born in February 1997). No matter that Enzo Ferrari always maintained that 'a driver loses speed when he becomes a father', Schumacher knew that, for him, the best was yet to come.

However, having the most powerful engine on the planet is worth nothing if all that power cannot be transferred to the tarmac. The engine side of the operation was working very well under Martinelli, aided by the arrival of Gilles Simon from Peugeot, but Montezemolo and Todt had to look outside when it came to designing the car. A year after Schumacher arrived, the team separately recruited Ross Brawn and Rory Byrne, the two men who had guided Schumacher to his first two titles with Benetton. Under the direction of Jean Todt, they stood alongside Paolo Martinelli and Gilles Simon, making up a technical caucus that would come to be known as the Ferrari 'dream team'. Over the years, they all extended their contracts to the end of 2006, putting together the most successful decade in the history of the Prancing Horse.

Along with Todt, these four men made the team. Todt's aim had always been to put the right people in the right job and both Brawn and Byrne matched his identikit picture, with the added advantage that they had worked with Schumacher before in a winning team. They knew that designing a car for Schumacher came with the added edge that he knew how to push it to its limit. However, Michael was not involved in recruiting either of them. Todt met with Brawn for the first time in May in Monaco and the deal was done over the next few months. By December, Ross was installed at Maranello.

'I had wanted to work at Ferrari and Ferrari had a job for me. On top of that, Schumacher was there. I knew him well, dating back to the days when I was a designer with Jaguar and he drove for Mercedes in the World Sports Car Championship. Then we worked together at Benetton and I realised that it was better to have him on your side rather than lined up against you.

'However, my decision to come to Maranello was mainly for Ferrari, for what it represented and for the programme that Todt had created around Schumacher.'

Ross Brawn is a calm and easygoing Mancunian, a Manchester United fan and a keen fisherman. He turns 50 on 24 November 2004, but has still not mastered the language of the country where he has lived since 1996. It's not a problem because everyone at Maranello and round about knows him well. He is the man who guides Schumacher from the pit wall and he is loved by every Ferrari fan.

During his career, Brawn has always left a good impression, even when he worked as a researcher in the atomic energy industry, the only period of his working life that has not revolved around engines. The rest of his time has been spent moving around English F1 teams. He began with Williams, where he spent eight years learning every aspect of his craft. Armed with this experience, he moved to Force as head of aerodynamics, then Arrows as chief designer, TWR where he ran the Jaguars in the world sports car championship and in 1991, he joined Benetton as technical director.

'As soon as I arrived at Maranello, I told myself the worst that could happen was to continue losing. I was taking no risks in signing an initial contract for three years. But, if things went well, it would be very gratifying. Winning with Ferrari would be a unique feeling.'

His first day was also the first time he had walked through the factory gates because his Benetton contract prevented him from going to Maranello prior to December.

'When I arrived, I was surprised. I expected the team to be at a lower level than it was, but the organisation looked good. Manufacturing was good, quality control was good and the team of mechanics led by Nigel Stepney was good. But in Formula 1, the slightest weakness makes the difference between excellence and mediocrity. What was really missing was our design department. Ferrari had the advantage of manufacturing everything in-house, from chassis to engine, but for the past few years, the chassis had been designed by John Barnard in England and this wiped out the advantage of having two groups collaborating and working together. Our aim was to do everything in-house, from design to building the complete car, not have the chassis come from one place and the engine from another. Total integration would be our strength. Therefore, the priority was to create the technical group.'

The task was to create a group to design the chassis and build it in the workshop right next door to the engine department and the test track where it would turn a wheel for the first time.

'Creating this group was my greatest challenge,' says Brawn. 'The rest was just a case of fine-tuning and tidying up. But I must admit, there was already a good base on which to build within Ferrari.'

Rory Byrne was born in Pretoria, South Africa on 10 January 1944 and, as a child, he liked to play with model gliders. The hobby would later help in his work, but on the way he won three world championships for hand-launched gliders. He got a degree in Chemical Engineering from the University of Johannesburg and immediately started work in the chemical industry, spending all his spare time working on a Ford Anglia. His passion for cars led him to quit his job and set up a car accessory shop. He started to design cars himself, building a Formula Ford that took second place in the 1972 South African Formula Ford championship. A year later, he moved to England, the heartland of motor sport.

In 1978, he joined Toleman, which later metamorphosed into Benetton. His first job was developing a car for the Toleman F2 team and he went on to design the Benetton in which Schumacher won the world championship. On the way, he was offered work by Colin Chapman, praised by Patrick Head, made an offer by Peugeot and, finally, approached by Jean Todt and Ferrari.

It took an 'indecent proposal' to get him to leave Thailand where he had embarked on a new life, setting up a scuba diving school in Phuket, but he was unable to resist the siren call. It was stronger than the lure of sun and sea in Thailand, the peace and quiet of the beaches and watching the sunset hand in hand with his fiancée.

'Todt called me and asked if I would be interested in working for Ferrari,' recalls Byrne. 'Ten days later I was in his office. When I said yes, we had not even spoken about money or contracts. Working for Ferrari, the most famous Formula 1 team in history, alongside Michael and Ross was a unique opportunity not to be missed.'

Montezemolo still recalls the day Byrne turned up, tanned and relaxed in a short-sleeved shirt, like someone who had just enjoyed a long holiday in the tropics. 'You will soon see that Maranello is much better than Phuket,' joked Montezemolo. Ten years down the line, those words ring true, as Ferrari's winning ways brought Byrne far more satisfaction than he could ever have dreamed of, even if he had run the best scuba diving school in the world.

Once installed at Maranello, in early February of 1997, Byrne quickly assessed the situation. 'Ferrari already had an excellent factory, with a strong structure and well-organised race team. However, what was missing was a research and development facility — in other words, everything John Barnard had in England. But it was his and not Ferrari's and his contract had not been renewed. The task was to set up a department that would form the basis of the Ferrari of the future.'

The starting point consisted of just a few designers and the small wind tunnel built in 1986, attached to the Gestione Sportiva. With that, they brought the heart of the design process back to Maranello and provided the opportunity to school a young team of engineers to work alongside Byrne and Brawn.

'The big challenge for '97, apart from winning with a car that wasn't mine or Ross's but had come from John Barnard, was to create the necessary structure to make the Formula 1 team competitive again.' The eyes of the world would be watching them.

The 1997 car started the season running about one second a lap slower than the Williams and ended the year on almost equal terms. A real research, development and production department was beginning to take shape around Byrne and it proved capable of lining up a 1998 car that was totally a Maranello product. New people were brought in, while existing talent within the factory was better deployed. It all led to the formation of the Ferrari we have today, with a group of around thirty people dedicated to design. They are supported by three other departments — structural analysis, run by Davide Terletti and responsible for the design of the chassis itself; research, headed by Ignazio Lunetta, Schumacher's former race engineer; and vehicle dynamics, led by Marco Fainello, which plays a vital role in the area of simulation and works with Bridgestone, as well as the aerodynamics team.

'We have created a working group that has grown with time and guarantees that Ferrari will be competitive even when I am back in Thailand,' says Byrne. 'I have always considered it part of my work to pass on my experience to the people at Ferrari, explaining how to organise research and how to design a race car. When I joined, Ferrari had not won the world championship for a very long time and there were no people capable of designing a winning car. Now we have a group who can do it without me.'

This group includes people who have seen their areas of responsibility increase year by year and who, one day, will be able to go it alone.

'Nowadays, I rarely sit at the drawing board although I still like to do some work on specific parts in 1:1 scale. My work is more that of coordinating the various groups and organising the departments. It's not like it was twenty years ago when I would sit and think about the car until I ran out of ideas. Now, everything is organised into work groups, each one of them with a set objective and a precise task. The end product is the result of the group's work as a whole.'

Back in '97, Ferrari was in the habit of shopping for engineers from other teams, but these days it is usually the other teams that court the men from Maranello. Ferrari has created its own very exclusive Silicon Valley around Maranello, which has given rise to the arrival of several specialist suppliers. This has meant that the team turns to England for very few specialist requirements.

'This is a vital advantage,' explains Ross Brawn, 'because when you have something made elsewhere, possibly by a supplier who also works for another team, it is easy for information to leak out.'

Normally, the basis for the design of a new car is the rulebook. The first step is to interpret the new rules, looking at all the angles. Then comes the real job of designing and five to six months later comes the finished product.

'Usually, I devote eighty to ninety per cent of my time from January to June to the new car, and then it's time to think about the following year's project. If there are no particular problems from September to October, time spent on the current car as it finishes the championship can go down to zero per cent,' explains Rory Byrne. As a rule, he does not attend the races, but is in constant contact with the team at the grands prix.

'It can happen that I get a call asking for help or advice. If I'm not in the factory, I can get there in five minutes.' That is just what happened in 1999, when he got the call from Malaysia to check on drawings for the barge boards, which were being measured to avoid disqualification after the race.

In the golden age, when the engineer Mauro Forghieri, father of Niki Lauda's car, was in charge, the Ferrari chassis and engine specialists had worked in isolation with no structure linking the two departments. Now, the flow of information between the departments is continuous. Engine and chassis men work together and the two groups are physically close to one another. It is no longer the case that everyone works solely on solving their own problems.

'Since Jean Todt's insistence on basing the entire technical project in Italy, we have created a strong and compact team that works in perfect harmony.' says Martinelli.

Ross Brawn confirms this fact. 'One of the strong points of Ferrari today,' he says, 'is that we design and build everything in-house. It might seem like a negative point compared to the way our rivals operate, but in fact it gives us an advantage. I've got friends in other teams and I've often heard Williams engineers complain about their BMW engine or BMW engineers complaining about the Williams chassis. That certainly doesn't happen here. Paolo Martinelli and I have our offices very close together and our groups exchange ideas on a daily basis to improve the final design.'

Every year, Ferrari builds around a hundred cylinder blocks and assembles around 250 engines. Development is continuous and there are at least three evolutions per season, while work on the following year's engine goes on at the same time. Development time is relatively lengthy. Initial design work takes place in the spring, bench and track testing gets under way over the autumn and winter, and a signed-off engine makes its race debut the following spring.

'Today, test benches are very sophisticated and produce ninety per cent of the answers we are looking for,' explains Martinelli. 'But track work is still indispensable because only when the engine is mated to the chassis do all eventualities and answers come to light.'

'My desk is no more than seven metres away from Luca Baldisserri's. That's the advantage of doing everything at Ferrari. If there are problems, we work to solve them together,' confirms Mattia Binotto, Schumacher's former engine man and current head of race engines. The best chassis in the world will never win without a good engine, just as the best engine in the world will never be able to use all its potential unless it is suited to the chassis. The opinion of the drivers is also taken into account.

'Michael, Rubens and the test drivers all help — some things only a driver can tell you,' reckons Byrne. 'But we aim to produce a car that is the quickest, whoever is at the wheel. It's not made to measure for Schumacher, even if Michael does always get a hundred per cent out of it.'

Today, there are calculation and simulation machines that can tell you how a car will go even before the engine is fired up, but then there are some things you can only learn on the track, when the driver is up against the opposition.

'Over the past few years, we have always managed to improve our cars. Each new car is better than the one from the previous year. The F2002 won fifteen out of nineteen races, while the F2003–GA took the championship at the final race, but that's simply because the opposition has become stronger and improved,' affirms Byrne.

There is no simulator that can tell you how easy the car is to drive and human feedback is essential for this.

'Now, when a new car takes to the track, we already know it is going to be quick. What we don't know is how reliable it will be and if it will be easy for the driver to take it to the limit,' continues Byrne.

'One special thing about Michael is that he can be very quick after just three laps. This means that usually it takes us a few laps only to understand how things are shaping up. And the same thing happens when we go to a new circuit,' adds Brawn.

The racetrack is Brawn's kingdom. He is the 'genius' of the pit wall. It is his role to run Schumacher and Barrichello and to determine race strategy, deciding when to call the drivers in for a pit stop to change tyres.

'Over a grand prix weekend, we have several briefings, usually three or four per day. They start on the Thursday and end on Sunday after the race, win or lose, because it is better to assess what happened in the heat of battle. A delay of two or three days can lose us precious time.

'We always start with a checklist and follow the same routine every time, starting with fuel loads and the type of tyre to use. There are ten to fifteen of us involved — the drivers, car engineers, engine specialists, Jean Todt, Stefano Domenicali, Paolo Martinelli and me. Having gone through the standard procedures, we move on to analysing any problems we had and any we might encounter. During meetings at the factory, we run off new checklists and, day by day, we go through the problems we experienced at the track, analysing the solutions using our technical resources and our own experience. This goes on until Sunday morning when we study the race strategy. At least, that was the case up to the end of 2002. New rules introduced for 2003 mean that in final qualifying, we have to run with enough fuel to start the race, so we start thinking about the race on Saturday mornings.

'It might seem as though we have a lot of meetings, but they are necessary to ensure we have covered all the angles, minimising the possibility of making any mistakes over the weekend. Concentration levels are high throughout the weekend because each one of us is aware of the importance of these meetings.'

On Sunday morning, on top of the official drivers' briefing, attended by all the drivers and the race director, team manager Stefano Domenicali runs an additional rules lesson.

'Along with Michael and Rubens, we go through the key points of the sporting regulations, the start procedure and possible interpretations of the rules. We go over the positioning of the white line that indicates the end of the pit-lane exit, the positioning of the marshals, the position of the start and finish lines, which are not always one and the same, and any other points.' It takes a few minutes but can prove vital, as Domenicali illustrates with this example.

'At the end of the Indianapolis race in 2003, Michael was accused of having overtaken under the yellow flags, but the video showed that, in fact, he had reached the point where the marshal had already finished waving the flag. Luck? No, because Michael knows that you are in the area of the yellow flags only when you pass in front of the marshal waving it. He knows where the marshals are located because he has been given that information in Sunday's briefing and he knows he can continue to go flat out up to that point. He is inquisitive and scrupulous and always wants to understand even the smallest detail.'

The meetings continue back in the factory, every Monday after a European grand prix, every Tuesday after races outside the Continent. These meetings involve around thirty to forty people and the president himself often attends, to praise or to push the team. This larger committee analyses the last race, plans the work and sets objectives for the next test sessions and races.

'In the seven years I have spent at Ferrari, these meetings have always been very constructive,' maintains Brawn. 'We are a company full of passion, but we always try to get the most out of these meetings. Then the detailed work is planned out in individual departmental meetings. Usually, at the end of the week, we go through what we call the performance briefing when we review our efforts after a week of track work if we have been testing, or in the factory. We focus our attention on the car's performance and how to get the most out of it in the forthcoming race.

'But this is not where we make the most important decisions. For example, at the start of the year, we have had to decide whether to run the new car or the one from the previous season. In these cases, the decision falls to Jean, Rory, Paolo and me and we study all the information before reaching a conclusion.' The big decisions rest with these four men.

Ferrari's success stems from these meetings. Briefings are not the sole prerogative of the men from Maranello, of course. All the other teams have them, too. However, the factor that has made Ferrari unbeatable over the past few years is definitely its strength as a group.

'Even in critical moments — and there have been plenty — we always try to resolve the problems ourselves, without revealing them to the outside world,' says Brawn. 'If someone makes a mistake, we stand by him, not letting one person take all the blame. The buck stops with Jean Todt, the drivers, Paolo Martinelli and me. We try to understand why the mistake has been made — maybe that person was under too much pressure or is not suited to his role. We have never shifted blame from one person to another and we have never punished anyone for making a mistake. It's not worth it as the strength of the group would suffer,' he maintains.

'If you want to know where our team spirit stems from, it comes from the '97, '98 and '99 seasons, when we lost three championships at the final round. If we had won the world championship right from 1997, we might not have become such a united group, with so much strength and the ability to react to any problems,' adds Byrne.

'We saw an example of this in 2003 when we managed to come through a difficult period without falling apart. We just knuckled down to the job, trying to understand how to solve the problems,' concludes Brawn, in an attempt to explain one of Ferrari's secrets.

Taking charge of how the race is run falls to Brawn because he is the one in radio contact with Schumacher and Barrichello during the event.

'When the race is straightforward, Michael talks a lot on the radio and gets me on edge, wanting to know everything that's going on — what's happening with his brother, Rubens and his rivals,' he says. 'Or he might have seen an accident on one of the giant screens around the track and want to know what happened. If he talks too much, I have to pull him up and get him concentrating again. However, if the race is close, if he has to push, the chat is reduced to a minimum. He asks for information but does not talk much.'

When it comes to testing, it is a different story. The race engineer, the engine specialist, the vehicle engineer and the chief mechanic on each car talk directly to the driver, with no need to go through Brawn. Schumacher deals with Dyer and Barrichello talks to Gabrielle Delli Colli. Brawn and Todt listen in and intervene only if they feel it necessary.

'Collaboration between our drivers is total. They work for the team and nothing about each other's set-up or strategy is secret. They both know what the other driver is working on,' says Brawn. Of course, Schumacher doesn't tell Barrichello what line to take in any particular corner, but there are no secrets when it comes to information. The two drivers are free to fight it out with equal equipment up to the point where the outcome of the world championship might be affected by the result, even though this might prove unpopular, as was the case in Austria in 2001 and 2002. But even in these cases, the situation never got out of hand and was kept under control by Todt and his men.

Taking Ferrari to the top required more than just having the right team. Equally important was having the right facilities. Here too, President Montezemolo always aims high. When the time came to design a new wind tunnel at the start of 1998, Montezemolo secured the services of Italian architect Renzo Piano, famous around the globe for his creativity. The Beaubourg in Paris, Osaka International Airport, Berlin's Potsdamer Platz and the Lingotto in Turin are all examples of his work. When it became obvious that the old wind tunnel was obsolete and not up to the demands of modern aerodynamic research, Montezemolo's thoughts turned to the man with whom he had already worked during the Italia '90 football World Cup. The finished product linked two facets of Ferrari — ties to Italy and the past on the one hand, and forward thinking and innovation on the other. This is no wind tunnel in a shed. It is a wind tunnel as a work of art, combining the highest technology inside with a highly aesthetic exterior.

'We tried to incorporate Enzo Ferrari's legacy of doing great things in a simple way,' explains Renzo Piano. The new wind tunnel allows work to be carried out on 50 per cent scale models and by simply changing a partition and some configuration settings, it can be used with a full-sized car.

'Now we can be sure that the figures we see from a wind-tunnel test tell us the truth right from the start, and good figures here mean the car will be good on the track,' explains Byrne.

The wind tunnel, which can simulate all types of set-up and movement — roll, yaw, pitch, steering and dynamic motion — is the focal point of what Montezemolo refers to as 'Research City', where everyone lives and breathes future progress. The wind tunnel was the first step in a complete rebuilding operation for the factory. The project, code named 'Formula Uomo' (Formula Man), has transformed Ferrari into the best working environment in Italy and indeed in the world. The quality of life for those working there is at its best whether it be in the industrial part of the factory or the Gestione Sportiva, which now benefits from the 'Nuova Logistica' (New Logistics) building where the F2003–GA was launched. This provides a logistical and transportation base for the Formula 1 cars and the team trucks. A new 'Complesso Direzionale' (Management Complex) will soon be operational, with offices and laboratories, as will the new Granturismo Paint Shop.

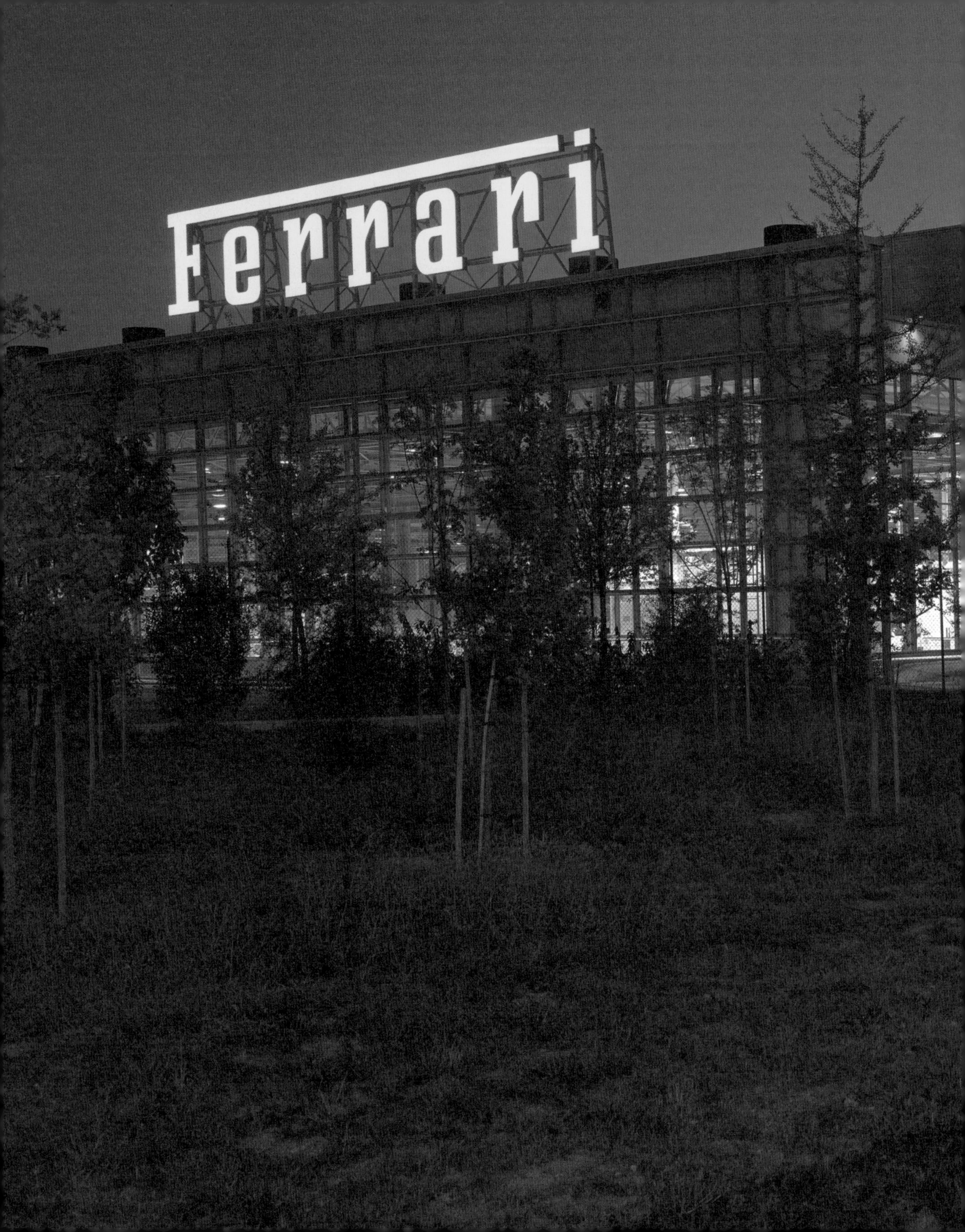
Ferrari

THE FERRARI FACTORY, MARANELLO

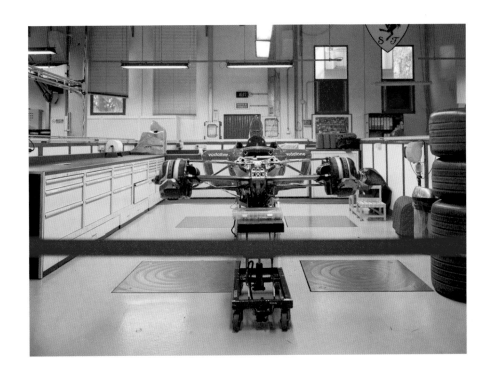

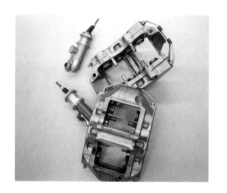

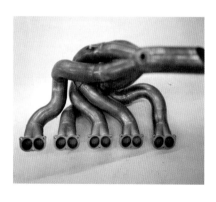

3 *THE TREND REVERSED*

Marching towards the world title

The year 1997 got off to the best possible start for Schumacher with the birth of his first child, Gina Maria, but it ended with one of the blackest days of his career, when he collided with Jacques Villeneuve at Jerez in the final race of the season. As a result of that incident, he was excluded from the championship classification. He would have finished second, just three points behind Villeneuve in his Williams-Renault.

During the season, Ferrari had continued to make progress, amassing five wins and over 100 points in the constructors' table, while Schumacher was virtual world champion until his coming together with Villeneuve.

'We lost the championship because of a driver error,' admit the men in red. But, ironically, it was this blow in the final race that gave rise to Ferrari's invincibility over the following years. Todt, Byrne, Brawn, Martinelli, Domenicali, Baldisserri and even Nigel Stepney and his boys are all agreed on this point. The ability to get over three bruising knocks from 1997 to 1999 helped forge a team that never gives up, one that remains united to fight back whenever the need arises.

'Michael definitely did a lot to create a sense of team spirit,' says Mattia Binotto, Schumi's engine engineer. 'He never put on any airs and graces, even though he is the driver and we are engineers and mechanics. As a group, we all get together without putting ourselves under pressure or creating tension. We have stuck together, never letting our little problems be known outside the team.'

The 1997 season appeared to get off to a good start in Australia, even if Schumacher did trail two seconds off Villeneuve's pole-setting pace in qualifying. With ten laps to go, Schumi closed in on David Coulthard, sat on his tail and tried to get past to take the lead, but from the pit wall came those words no driver ever wants to hear — 'Come in. Refuel.'

'What? Are you talking to me?'

'Yes, Michael. Come in. Come in immediately.'

'Is there no other way?'

'No, come in. You're out of fuel.'

That one additional stop allowed Coulthard and victory to slip away — the race marked a return to the winner's enclosure for McLaren, after forty-nine races, and Mercedes, for the first time since 1955 — but deep down, Schumacher knew the car could do it and that Ferrari was on the up and up.

'Fingers crossed, I predict a good season and we will be in the running for the title,' he declared.

The Brazilian and Argentinian races failed to deliver but Imola brought another second place.

'I feel that we are on the pace and wins are within our grasp,' Schumacher was quoted as saying.

Instead of flying home on his private jet, he stayed at Maranello. Enzo Ferrari's former office at the Fiorano circuit had been transformed into Schumacher's personal base, complete with bedroom, bathroom and gym. Staying there meant he could be up bright and early ready for testing, and at the end of the day he could relax playing football with the lads. Schumacher is like that — fastidious and meticulous in every detail. That Sunday, he sensed a win was not far off and the next race would be in Monaco, one of his favourite circuits. He was keen to start getting the car ready. The Scuderia had not won in Monaco since the days of Gilles Villeneuve, back in 1981.

Schumacher qualified second, splitting the two Williams of Heinz-Harald Frentzen and Villeneuve. The big question was the weather. Grey clouds massed around the hilltop castle. Would it rain or not? At the time, the team relied on two weather forecasting services, one Italian and one French. Naturally, they did not quite agree. The former spoke of heavy showers in the afternoon, the latter predicted a 90 per cent chance of rain after two in the afternoon. There were some at Ferrari, including press officer Claudio Berro, who preferred to believe in the accuracy of the local fishermen. In the end, Schumacher opted for intermediate tyres and wet-weather settings. Williams' forecasters expected the sun to reappear and chose dry tyres.

Just before the start, it began to rain and the scene was set. Schumi raced through the puddles, rapidly pulling away for a six-second lead over Giancarlo Fisichella, while the Williams pair were in crisis. Schumi continued to fly until running wide at Ste Devote corner on lap fifty-three. Watching on the TV screens, Montezemolo came close to a heart attack, while Todt, with no nails left, switched to chewing his fingers. However, the man himself kept his cool, controlled his F310B, just missed the barriers and after an amazing and deliberate spin, was back on course as though nothing had happened.

He went on to triumph, giving Ferrari its first win at Monaco for sixteen years, and propelling himself and the team to the top of both classifications. It was 11 May, a significant day in the Prancing Horse's history — on the very same date back in 1947, Franco Cortese raced the 125 at Piacenza, marking Ferrari's race debut.

After Monaco, Schumacher won in Canada, France and, at the end of the summer, Belgium on his favourite track. He also won in Japan in the penultimate round of the season. In this race, Villeneuve's championship chances were dealt a serious blow when the stewards docked him the two points he scored over a yellow flag incident.

Before that, the older Schumacher had a contretemps with his brother Ralf at the start of the Luxembourg Grand Prix at the Nurburgring and, as it turned out, this cost Michael dear in the classification table.

At the start of the season's finale, the European Grand Prix at Jerez de la Frontera on 26 October, Schumacher was on seventy-eight points, one more than Villeneuve, his only rival for the title. With the championship up for grabs, even Jody Scheckter, the last Ferrari champion, came to watch the action. Shops were stocking celebration hats and shirts, and the President's pilot had already filed a flight plan.

Qualifying produced an incredible result, with three drivers all setting the same time, down to a thousandth of a second. Villeneuve, Schumacher and Frentzen all posted 1 minute 21.072 seconds. Apparently, there is a one in 223 million chance of this happening. Having been the first to set the time, Villeneuve was to start from pole, with Schumacher alongside him and Frentzen behind.

It had been a very hot week leading up to the final showdown and Villeneuve, always ready to speak his mind, upped the temperature with a throwaway remark. 'I'm worried about a collision at the start, or a sudden change of line,' he said. On the Saturday morning, he almost came to blows with Eddie Irvine, Schumacher's team-mate, after an incident on the track.

The race began very well for Schumacher. He immediately got ahead of Villeneuve to lead going into the first corner and he kept that lead, even during the two pit stops. With twenty-one laps to go to the chequered flag, the title was in sight.

'After the second stop, we began to tell him that Villeneuve was closing,' recalls Ross Brawn, 'but Michael replied that we should stay calm. Everything was OK.'

Villeneuve continued to close — 2.5 seconds after his pit stop, 1.026 next time round, then 0.385. The Williams-Renault was looming large in the Ferrari wing mirrors and at Dry Sack corner, Villeneuve suddenly dived down the inside, catching Schumacher completely by surprise. Schumacher, desperately trying to close the door on the Williams, hit it. It was a disaster. The Ferrari finished the race in the gravel, while Villeneuve kept going. In the end, Mika Hakkinen won in the McLaren but Villeneuve had the title that had always eluded his father, Gilles.

Schumacher was in no hurry to get back to the pits as the incident came under scrutiny. Immediately, comparisons were made with the 1994 race in Adelaide when, as a Benetton driver, he hit the barriers and was then hit by Damon Hill's Williams, which was so damaged that the British driver was forced to retire.

Although Schumacher tried to justify his actions, no one would defend him, with the exception of his team, united in defeat as they would have been in victory. Even on that disappointing night in Jerez, Luca di Montezemolo was keen to stress the Ferrari ethic — never blame one another, win or lose together.

The President did not cancel his flight to Spain. It had been planned so he could celebrate with the team but it turned into a journey of consolation. He played the role of lightning conductor, taking the flak away from Schumacher and the team, while trying to get them to look to the future, seeking out a positive side to this defeat.

'This was supposed to be a transition year, but we ended up taking the title fight down to the wire,' he emphasised, dismissing the idea that the Jerez affair could have further repercussions.

Schumacher's attempt at penance began in the bar of the hotel where he met Villeneuve to try to explain things, but his comments did little to appease his critics.

'Jacques made an unexpected move on me, a move that I would define as very optimistic. I braked as hard as I could and he used my car to slow down, to finish his braking and not go off the track. He did well to catch me out and he popped out from nowhere. I tried to close the door, but it was already too late and we touched. Unfortunately, it went well for him and badly for me,' explained the Ferrarista on Sunday night.

On the Monday after the race, the FIA president, Max Mosley, announced that Schumacher would be called before a disciplinary hearing. It was not enough that Ferrari had called a press conference at Maranello, putting Schumacher in the spotlight for the TV crews to explain the accident and to apologise to Villeneuve once again, and to the world at large.

'It was only the next day that I understood what had happened. In future, I will react differently to certain situations. I spoke to Villeneuve and he listened without rancour. I wanted to win the world championship, but I got it wrong,' said Schumacher.

The hearing took place on 11 November at the offices of the RAC (Royal Automobile Club) where the FIA World Council were meeting. The worry was that the driver could be disqualified from some of the following year's races, which would have seriously compromised his championship chances. In the end, nothing so harsh came of it. His name was scrubbed from the results of the 1997 championship, his second place removed from the record books, although the team kept the points counting towards the constructors' championship. In addition, Schumacher would carry out 'community service' by helping with the FIA's road safety campaign. Given what might have been, he got off lightly. All that mattered to Ferrari and their driver was that the future had not been compromised.

'Schumacher makes one mistake in the year, but when he does, everyone talks about it,' commented Gianni Agnelli.

After a period when Formula 1 had been dominated by sons of famous fathers, with Damon Hill and Jacques Villeneuve becoming champions, Mika Hakkinen now came forward to stake his claim. Schumacher regarded McLaren's Finnish driver as one of his strongest rivals.

On 7 January 1998, against the Hollywood-style backdrop of the Renzo Piano-designed wind tunnel, the F300 was unveiled. The message from the stage was clear and to the point — this time we need to win. In truth, Schumi and Ferrari came very close but six wins, three pole positions and a record total of 133 points scored in the constructors' championship were not enough. Schumacher and Ferrari both had to settle for second place, beaten by Mika Hakkinen and McLaren-Mercedes. That was a shame — victory in either or both would have been the perfect way to celebrate the centenary of the birth of the company founder, Enzo Ferrari.

Schumacher was again in the running for the title right up to the last race, the Japanese Grand Prix, arriving at Suzuka four points behind his rival. But the championship was not decided at the final race, where Schumacher had a technical problem at the start. The key moment of 1998 occurred at the Belgian Grand Prix on 30 August.

It was a special day for Ferrari because the team was celebrating taking part in its 600th grand prix. A huge crash involving thirteen cars led to the stewards ordering a re-start, but second time around the race appeared to be going well for Schumacher. It was raining hard and in those conditions, he was unbeatable. After twenty-four laps he already had a thirty-seven second lead over the second-placed car and, more importantly, he was effectively leading the championship. The ten points on offer for the win would put him ahead of Hakkinen, who had retired in the early stages. But then, on lap twenty-five, with visibility down to virtually zero, Schumacher speared the back of Coulthard's McLaren at high speed, which left the Ferrari with just three wheels and put the German in a terrible rage.

'You tried to kill me,' he screamed at Coulthard, trying to grab him.

'You're an animal,' shouted back the Scotsman.

It took a long time for the situation to cool down and for Coulthard and Schumacher to make their peace.

Once again, Schumacher's actions came under scrutiny but this time opinion was divided. Some sided with him, accusing Coulthard of being the 'assassin', while others felt Schumacher had gone too far and taken needless risks in terrible weather, especially as Hakkinen was already out of the running. The end result was that those lost ten points cost Schumacher the title in his final battle with Hakkinen.

Guilty or innocent, that's the way Schumacher is — never happy unless he is giving his utmost and pushing to the limit. This attitude to the sport has furnished some incredible results, beyond the reach of other drivers, but there are times when he misses out on a golden opportunity, which is what happened at a rain-soaked Spa.

There are still some doubts about Coulthard's actions. Obviously, he did not deliberately risk his life trying to be hit, but neither did he do as much as he could to let his rival pass him. Later, the McLaren driver apologised to Michael.

'It was not the first overtaking move I had made in the wet and it would not have made any sense to come up behind the McLaren so quickly. I had been trying to pass him for two laps, but he did all he could to make the move as difficult as possible. The marshals were waving blue flags, but he continued to block me,' recalls Schumacher.

'Michael asked me over the radio to go to Ron Dennis to get his driver to move over,' adds Todt.

'Luckily, I braked and it ended all right. I could have killed myself by hitting the McLaren,' concludes Schumacher.

Schumacher's reaction was certainly out of character. Once back in the pits, he immediately headed for the McLaren garage, chased by Stefano Domenicali, who was trying to calm him down. Michael wanted an instant explanation from Coulthard, believing that what had happened on the track could not easily be dismissed as a racing incident. Todt had to intervene to pour oil on troubled waters. Looking at the bigger picture, the missing ten points for the win would count heavily in championship terms and it is fair to say that Michael lost the title at Spa rather than at Suzuka, a few weeks later.

Earlier in the season, there had been an unforgettable afternoon at Monza, when the Italian Grand Prix ended with a one-two finish for the red team for the first time in a decade.

'This is the Ferrari I have always dreamed of,' enthused Montezemolo. But it was not enough to take the championship. At the Nurburgring, Hakkinen was back to his winning ways and he did it again in the final round at Suzuka, where Schumacher's engine cut out at the start.

'When I selected first gear, the engine cut out because the clutch engaged. It was nothing to do with the tension of the moment but just one of those things that can happen. However, we didn't lose the championship here, but earlier in the season, when McLaren were stronger than us,' was Schumacher's pertinent analysis.

Morale did not falter even though the title was still a dream. Year after year, it came close then slipped away. It seemed like a curse.

'I hope not. I promised the title in three years, but we have not managed it,' said Schumacher to Montezemolo. But Schumacher and Ferrari continued to believe. Indeed, on 17 July, at the height of the championship tussle, the knot binding Michael and the Reds had been extended to the end of 2002. There was talk of over $30 million per season, but it was not the money that mattered. Schumacher still firmly believed in Ferrari's mission, and with the target looming ever closer, he knew he could build a golden future with this team.

TESTING AT FIORANO

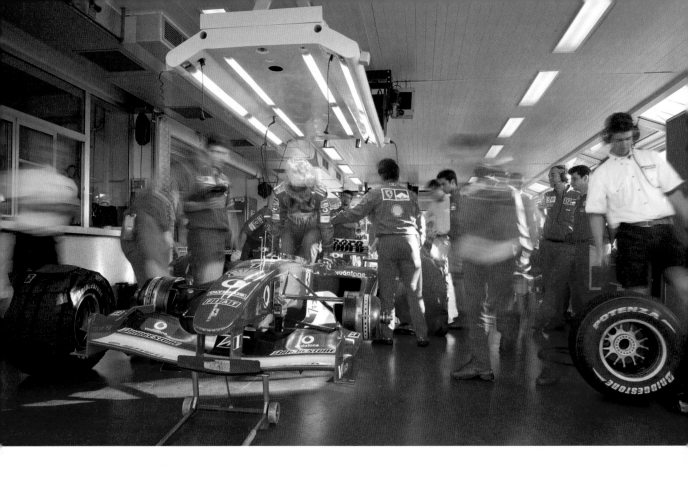

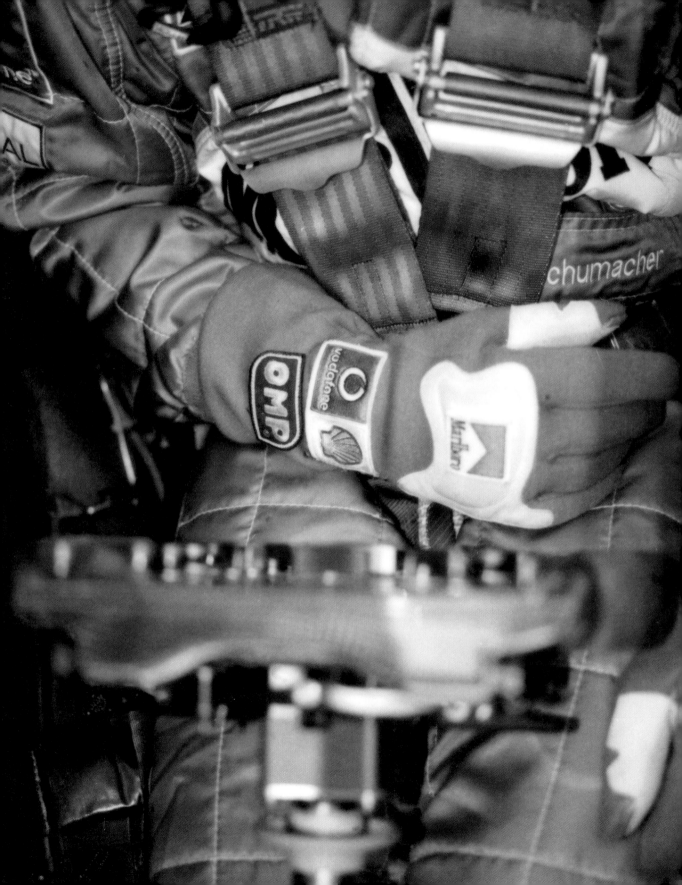

4

1999 – FIRST BLOOD TO THE TEAM

The constructors' title is in the bag

On 30 January 1999, the F399 was unveiled to the world in a marquee at the Fiorano circuit. Unusually, all 450 employees of the Gestione Sportiva were on hand to salute the latest Ferrari racer because the management wanted to give centre stage to everyone who would work throughout the year in support of Schumacher and Irvine. The men and women of the Gestione Sportiva, dressed in red and proud to be part of the world-famous team, provided the backdrop to what, over the years, had become a traditional ceremony, as the new car was displayed.

'Ferrari has not won the drivers' world championship for twenty years so it is even more eagerly anticipated,' was Gianni Agnelli's pithy remark.

'We will not be unbeatable, but we will definitely be one of the teams to beat,' Ross Brawn was keen to assure everyone as the dustsheet came off the F399.

Although it looked very much like the previous year's F300, it was a completely new design. The rear end had been changed and the sides had been heavily reworked in the wind tunnel. There was a significant weight saving, with talk of 20 kilos having been lopped off. It also had a new 048 engine and electronically controlled hydraulics. In common with all the other teams that year, the car ran on Bridgestone tyres. While striving for perfection, the thirty Prancing Horse aerodynamics experts, led by Nicholas Tombazis, had ensured that the wind tunnel was in use sixteen hours a day, from seven in the morning to eleven at night, except for Sundays.

'I am very motivated about the coming season. For me, Ferrari is like a family and all our fans are a part of it,' said Michael Schumacher, unexpectedly speaking in Italian. 'It's harder for me to say these few words of Italian than to do a qualifying lap,' he confessed.

He could not wait to get on the track to try the new machine. The engine was eventually fired up on the 5 February, the car completing just a handful of laps before dusk fell on the Fiorano track.

The first setback came the next day – while Schumacher was travelling at a heady 280 km/h, the rear wing flew off, the car spun and he ended up off the track. These things can happen with a brand new car and the incident had no effect on the driver's confidence.

'We have to do a lot of kilometres, but first impressions are good,' he confirmed.

The first race of the year was run in Australia on 7 March and Ferrari won — the first time the team had been victorious in the opening round since 1989 — but it was not Schumacher's name on the winner's trophy. The German started the season in the same way he had finished the previous one. He was unable to get off the line for the formation lap and had to start from the back of the grid. Then he suffered an electrical problem that involved a visit to the pits to change the steering wheel. All hopes were pinned on Irvine and after eighty-one grands prix starts, Eddie finally achieved every driver's dream, taking the first Formula 1 win of his career — and at the wheel of a Ferrari to boot.

'Sometimes the tortoise can beat the hare,' he philosophised, but that first win came to change his perspective and as his best-ever season progressed, he began to harbour thoughts of leaving Ferrari, giving up his role as a permanent squire to Schumacher and enjoying life as a lead driver. 'Having tasted victory, I realise that I can no longer deal with moving over to let my team-mate through,' he admitted.

Schumacher had to make do with a far from satisfactory eighth place. Not even a second-place finish behind Hakkinen five weeks later in Brazil gave cause for satisfaction. Irvine, fifth in Brazil, still led the championship, but no one read much into this. There was still much to do to turn the F399 into a winner.

'There is no specific problem, but we have to make up the odd hundredths of a second in every area and we also have to learn to make better use of the Bridgestone tyres, which are new to us,' explained Ross Brawn.

The heavy workload bore fruit in the San Marino Grand Prix at Imola. Hakkinen was on pole again, for the third consecutive time that season, but the Finn's race ended on lap seventeen when he crashed into the pit wall. He had been dominating the race and took all the blame for the incident although there was talk of a problem with the differential on his McLaren. That left his team-mate Coulthard in the lead, but Schumacher was going flat-out, transforming the race into one long qualifying session with perfectly precise and speedy pit stops, and he came in ahead of Coulthard in front of a sea of red flags.

The victory was built on driver ability and team strategy. Ross Brawn controlled the situation perfectly from the pit wall, knowing he could count on Schumacher to put the strategy to good use.

'When I was on the slowing-down lap after crossing the finish line, I felt incredible emotions,' said Schumacher just after the race. 'Happiness made up for all the bitterness of the past few weeks. Seeing all the fans with our flags was amazing. When people ask me why I joined Ferrari, I tell them about these moments and everyone understands.'

Schumacher took the lead in the championship at Imola, and went on to extend it in Monaco. Hakkinen was once again on pole but Schumacher shot off the line ahead of him and was uncatchable from then on. It was his fourth victory in the streets of the Principality and, with Irvine following him home in second place, marked an historic one-two finish for Ferrari, the first at this circuit in the team's fifty years in the sport. It was also an historic moment for Schumacher as his sixteenth victory for Ferrari meant he had won more races with them than any other driver, beating Niki Lauda's previous record of fifteen — just the first of many records that Schumacher and the Scuderia would establish in this golden period. Schumacher now had a twelve-point lead over Hakkinen and was six points clear of team-mate Irvine, but there was no time for euphoria.

'We must keep our feet on the ground and keep pushing.' This phrase has become something of an obsession for Montezemolo, Todt, the engineers and the drivers and it illustrates Ferrari's mindset during these years. Win or lose, the Mondays after a race always follow the same pattern – work, work and more work. If another team has done better, the aim is to catch them up. In the event of a win it's a case of ensuring a repeat performance. Everyone sings from the same hymn sheet, never resting on laurels, always chasing perfection.

In Formula 1, there is no place for complacency after a victory. In fact, it took Hakkinen just two races to turn the situation round. With wins in Spain and Canada he made up sixteen points on Schumacher, who finished third in Barcelona and out of the running in Montreal, his car parked in the wall at the last corner. Schumacher got it wrong at the same place that had claimed the chances of two other world champions, Hill and Villeneuve.

'It's my first mistake of the season and I hope it is also my last,' he confessed. Admitting his mistakes and not trying to pass the blame is another strong point in the relationship between Schumacher and Ferrari.

In Magny-Cours, the team got it wrong, making a rare mistake in the pits. When the heavens opened, Irvine was the first of the Ferrari drivers to come in for rain tyres, which could have been the winning move if the mechanics had not fumbled in finding the right ones. Irvine was delayed in the pits for forty seconds, an eternity in Formula 1 terms. It was a missed opportunity.

The rain also delivered Schumacher a fatal blow as his steering wheel began to malfunction and he dropped down the order. At this point, team tactics came into play – Ferrari asked Irvine to protect Schumacher by not passing him, so that he at least managed to come home fifth, safeguarding a precious extra point. It seemed the right move at the time, given that Schumacher had more points than Irvine, even though Hakkinen now had an eight-point lead. With hindsight, it might have been better to leave the extra points with Eddie.

However, no one could have predicted what happened on 11 July at Silverstone. At 1.03 p.m., Michael Schumacher ended up in the tyre wall on the outside of Stowe corner. The telemetry revealed that at the point of impact he had been travelling at 107 km/h. The nose of the Ferrari buried itself in the tyres and broke off. It happened because of 'an unexpected drop in pressure in the rear brake circuit, caused by a failure of a bleed nipple on the left rear caliper', according to the official statement released from Maranello two days later.

The TV cameras zoomed in on Schumacher trying to get out of the cockpit but unable to do so. He had to wait for the rescue crews and it took nine minutes to extricate him. As he was carried to a waiting ambulance, he raised his arm to indicate he was all right. He was taken to Northampton General Hospital by helicopter but before then contact was made with his wife, Corinna, to reassure her about Michael's condition.

His life was not in danger but the tibia and fibula in his right leg were broken and surgery was required to insert a plate. The procedure went ahead after Jean Todt had spoken with close friend and respected surgeon Professor Saillant. Michael had intended to get back in the cockpit as quickly as possible, maybe even for the Hungarian Grand Prix. Unfortunately, his broken leg still caused him too much pain and there was no return in Budapest. After a minor operation in a Swiss hospital, Michael was back on track at Mugello on 20 August. With eight hours and sixty-five laps — around 340 kilometres — at the wheel of an F399 under his belt, it seemed likely that a return to competition could be pencilled in for the Belgian Grand Prix, but it did not happen. Another trial run took place at Monza, with a view to a return for the Italian Grand Prix, but a handful of laps was enough for Michael to know it was not possible. Rumours began to circulate that he would not race again until the following season and Michael even confirmed that this was the most likely scenario.

During the first week of October, Ferrari organised a test session at Fiorano, in preparation for the Malaysian Grand Prix. For a third time, Michael strapped himself in to his car to assess his physical condition. The test went well and was followed up with a three-way conversation between the driver, Montezemolo and Todt. If Michael was up to driving in a grand prix, he would be giving Ferrari a decisive helping hand in the championship battle, with Irvine locked in a duel with Hakkinen for the drivers' title and the team in the running to beat McLaren for the constructors' championship. The ball was firmly in Schumacher's court. He did not disappoint and set off to race in Sepang.

At the mid-point of the season, Eddie had the same points total as Schumacher, eight less than Hakkinen. At Silverstone, with Schumi in hospital, Irvine wasted a great chance when he overshot his marker at the pit stop. Hakkinen had retired after losing a badly fitted wheel and, but for those few seconds, Eddie could have emerged ahead of Coulthard and won. As it was, he had to settle for second place, which did at least allow him to close on Hakkinen. However, the best was yet to come.

Schumacher's accident coincided with Fiat's centenary celebrations in Turin. Naturally, Montezemolo was not in the best frame of mind that day, but he was obliged to take part in the event, while staying in constant contact with Todt. They had to think of whom they should get to replace Michael. The most obvious choice was Luca Badoer, the Scuderia's official test driver. The Italian driver knew the team and the car, but they decided that, all things considered, it would put too much pressure on him. Jean Alesi's name was also in the frame, but the Frenchman was certainly not the sort to act as Irvine's water carrier. In the end, Montezemolo and Todt settled on Mika Salo, who had been without a drive since the start of the season. The Finn came to Maranello on the Monday evening after the British Grand Prix and it did not take long to reach an agreement. The first thing Salo had to do was postpone his wedding to his Japanese fiancée, Noriko. It had been due to take place on 25 July, but Salo would have another duty to fulfil that day at Austria's Zeltweg circuit.

Austria and Germany turned into the 'Eddie Irvine Show'. Eddie walked away with two firsts and the championship lead, and Ferrari woke up to the fact they could win without Schumacher. It gave the team a confidence boost as it dawned on them that all was not lost, despite the misfortune that had befallen their number one driver.

In Austria, Irvine made the most of a collision between Hakkinen and Coulthard. In Germany, he profited when Hakkinen's right rear tyre disintegrated as he came into the Motodrom and Salo moved over to let him take the lead and win – a perfect example of the sort of teamwork that Irvine had to produce when Schumacher was around. This was Eddie's moment, when he was unexpectedly transformed from squire into knight in Schumacher's absence. There were suggestions that someone within Ferrari – reading between the lines it was Todt who was implicated – was none too happy about the Irishman's successes. Adding fuel to the gossipmongers' fire was the introduction in Austria of a rotation system for team members to go up on to the podium to receive the constructors' trophy. When Nigel Stepney joined Eddie for the prize-giving ceremony, some people took this as a sign that Todt was distancing himself from Michael's team-mate, especially those among the press who were not particularly well disposed towards the Frenchman.

At Hockenheim, Irvine dedicated the win to Salo, even handing him the winner's trophy on the podium. During the race, there had been clear-cut instructions from the pit wall. Salo, who had been leading, had to make way for Eddie to bring home a great one-two finish. The Finn obeyed without the slightest hesitation in a show of true professionalism. This was no minor sacrifice, given that it would have been the first and only time in his career that he would have won a grand prix.

'I would have liked to play deaf and pretend I had not heard, but I could not do it. When I signed for Ferrari, I accepted the rules of the game. I knew that Eddie was in with a chance of the championship and the team wanted to do all it could. These four points were too important for his position,' explained the Finn.

After two wins from two races the reaction of the 'Schumiless ones' was incredible and unforeseen.

'The difference is that when Michael is on track, we engineers are under less pressure because we know that he is a cut above and a reference point for the rest of us,' explained Ross Brawn, who worked out the winning strategy. 'Without him, it's up to us to find that half second. Eddie is doing an excellent job.'

Irvine's contract was due to expire at the end of the season and Ferrari had already decided to find another team-mate for Michael. Eddie was thus able to accept a princely offer from Jaguar, which included not only number one status, but also a huge amount of money. Between Silverstone and Zeltweg, Montezemolo and Todt had a meeting at the Fiera di Bologna with the Irish driver and his manager, Enrico Zanarini. It was an opportunity to clear the air and to re-emphasise the faith the Ferrari management had in Eddie for the rest of the season, now that he had assumed the role of lead driver in the team.

Ferrari's choice was Rubens Barrichello, who had already been considered at the end of 1995, when, as it happened, the Brazilian was Irvine's team-mate at Jordan. From the start of the year, Barrichello had begun to rack up some impressive results for the Stewart team and the official announcement was made just prior to the Italian Grand Prix in September.

Eddie Irvine now had an eight-point lead over Hakkinen, with six races remaining. From his home in Switzerland, Schumacher sent him his blessing and support.

'When I come back, I'll work for Eddie. I'll settle for the number two role because I believe Eddie deserves that, having done so much for me in the past.' It was a significant statement from the champion and he was able to fulfil his promise in the final two races of the season, in Malaysia and Japan.

Until then, Eddie had to fend for himself, albeit with help from Salo and the team. His most valued ally was Luca Baldisserri, his race engineer. Baldisserri's knack of interpreting Eddie's needs and pinpointing the best set-up was so well honed that Ferrari decided to put him to work on Schumacher's car the following year. Baldisserri also had a personal interest to consider. Back in Australia, before the championship got under way, he was regarded as mad for having bet a million lire on Irvine taking the title. He stood to pocket a cool hundred million lire.

However, in Hungary, Irvine made a mistake and lost a certain second place. Then in Belgium, he lost out again in a straight fight with Hakkinen, who thus moved ahead in the table by a single point. In fact, things could have been much worse but for the actions of Ron Dennis and the McLaren team — Hakkinen finished second, beaten by his team-mate, Coulthard, who thus deprived the Finn of four important points. Irvine said thank you. This result also meant that McLaren-Mercedes crept ahead of Ferrari in the constructors' championship for the first time that season.

At Monza, on the home track, Eddie had everything to play for. There was talk of Schumacher returning, and 12,000 tifosi turned up to watch him test the car, waving 'Schumi + Irvine = Ferrari Champions' banners, and they really believed it. It took just five laps for him to realise that the unforgiving kerbs of the Lombardy track were too much for his leg to bear.

'I came here to get ready to race in the Italian Grand Prix, but unfortunately that will not happen. I can't do it. My leg hurts too much and I can only manage a few laps at a time. There is no point in kidding myself. I'll just have to keep on trying. I'll skip Monza and the European Grand Prix and then we'll see.'

You only needed to look at his face to see he was telling the truth. It was the first time he had come face to face with the press since the accident. He had made a television appearance from home, which was shown to the crowd at the German Grand Prix, before trying out his leg at Mugello, but that had taken place behind closed doors. Here at Monza, he made himself available to answer questions, looking back at what really happened on 11 July at Stowe corner.

'When I think about what happened to me, I realise how lucky I was to have only broken a leg. Ten years ago, I would have been knocking on the gates to see Saint Peter. A couple of minutes after the accident, I did think about giving up racing, but already before the race at Hockenheim I had begun to talk to Jean Todt about improvements on the car. I was already dreaming of coming back. I realised that racing is in my blood and I cannot do without it.'

He had a curt answer to insinuations that he was not coming back because he did not want to help Irvine.

'I drive for Ferrari and Eddie does too. I'll do whatever I'm asked to do by the team, whatever is in the best interests of the team, not just Eddie. I have already said I would have no problem letting him pass me if the situation arises.'

'Michael would have helped me, but now that won't happen,' said Irvine, who still believed he could be champion. 'There's no point crying. We just have to forget about it and give it our best shot.'

Ferrari was off form in Monza qualifying, with Salo sixth and Irvine eighth. Hakkinen was on pole and charged off into the distance. Ten points and a handhold on the title were within his grasp, but on lap thirty, while leading, he went off the track at the first chicane and stopped in the gravel. Climbing out of the

McLaren and sinking to his knees under a tree, he burst into tears — sweet tears for Eddie Irvine, who finished with a point, enough to put him back in contention with three races remaining.

Mathematically, Frentzen and Coulthard were also in with a chance, but realistically they were not in the running, even if the two of them did line up on the front row of the grid for the next round, the European Grand Prix at the Nurburgring. It was yet another race to forget for Ferrari. The team made a complete mess of Irvine's pit stop, costing him an eternity, or twenty-eight seconds to be precise. He was left sitting on the jacks with just three wheels, as the fourth one had gone missing.

'Get the rain tyres ready,' Irvine instructed over the radio as he prepared to come in on lap twenty-one. 'No, no, give me dries,' he shouted a few moments later.

For a moment, it was total confusion in the pits, resulting in one of the four wheels — the right rear — going missing, left in a corner. It was a serious mistake that cost the team dear. Even if Irvine had not won, he would have finished ahead of Hakkinen and thus regained the championship lead. In the end, he finished seventh, out of the points, while his title rival came home fifth, picking up a valuable two. With two races to go, Irvine was two points behind Hakkinen, so there was still everything to play for, even if there had been too many lost opportunities.

Malaysia marked the long-awaited return of Schumacher but before he could get back behind the wheel, he had to undergo two final tests. Michael had to jump up and down on his right leg and also prove he could extricate himself from the cockpit in under ten seconds. The tests went off without a hitch. Corinna, who had watched the proceedings, gave him her blessing.

'If Michael's happy, then I'm happy too,' she said.

No need to add that the happiest person of all was Jean Todt, who was delighted to see his man back on track, especially as it meant that there was now a very good chance of at least taking the constructors' title.

This was Formula 1's first visit to Malaysia. The Sepang track is close to Kuala Lumpur airport. Where ninety hectares of jungle once thrived, the Malaysians have built one of the most modern race circuits in the world, with a track as wide as a six-lane motorway. It was ideal for Schumacher, who was keen to prove that he was still the best.

'I'm here to help Ferrari win the constructors' world championship. I'm not bothered about Eddie, but if I find myself in the lead, I'll let him pass,' he said, repeating the promise he made a few months earlier. This time, he had the opportunity to be true to his word.

One hundred and two days after the accident at Silverstone, he was back in action on a grand prix weekend. Out of the cockpit, he still limped slightly, but at the wheel, it was the same old Schumi, maybe even better than before.

During first practice, he had a small slide and felt a shiver run down his spine.

'When I thought I might be going off the track, I thought of the accident and the tyre wall, but it only lasted a moment. Apart from that, I just tried to learn the circuit, find the right set-up and improve lap by lap,' he said. Naturally, the next day, he took pole position. The king was back.

In the race, he did as he pleased. He was totally dominant and twice he moved over for Irvine, maintaining station behind him, riding shotgun in case of a McLaren attack and handing the Irishman the win and ten points. Eddie headed for Japan with a four-point lead over Hakkinen, and the team led by the same margin over McLaren-Mercedes.

But Malaysia had a sting in its tail for Ferrari. While Irvine was already on a plane to Hong Kong, bedlam broke out at the circuit. Schumacher and Irvine had been disqualified and victory handed to Hakkinen, virtually assuring him of the title with one race to go. It was all down to a matter of millimetres in the measurement of the Ferrari barge boards, deemed illegal by Jo Bauer, the FIA technical delegate. Ten millimetres, one centimetre — it looked as though Ferrari were about to lose it all for this tiny discrepancy.

'After the chequered flag, our cars went into parc ferme for checking,' explained Jean Todt. 'The scrutineers noticed a problem with the side deflectors. We have not yet been able to ascertain why the part does not conform to the regulations, whether it is a design fault or a problem in the way it was fitted. But we can assure you that this difference carries absolutely no performance advantage and we are ready to prove that in the wind tunnel. We have nine or ten parts like this and they are all the same. We used them in the European Grand Prix, but they were not found to be at fault there.'

There were rumours of a McLaren tip-off, and that Ron Dennis's team had been keeping the information since the end of the race at the Nurburgring. Certainly, someone must have suggested to Bauer and his colleagues that they check those particular parts. Naturally, Ferrari announced that they were appealing against the disqualification. There was no other possible course of action. Now it was up to the engineers and lawyers to win the race all over again in a Paris courtroom.

In the meantime, Todt had returned to Italy to explain the situation to Montezemolo. 'It's down to the team boss to take responsibility for what happened,' said Todt. 'We believe this disqualification is unjust and we will do all in our power to prove it.' The appeal was put together in less than a week, with the help of two lawyers, Henry Peter and Jean Pierre Martel. In London, Bernie Ecclestone declared that it would be absurd for the championship to be decided by a mistake by someone working in the factory. In Maranello, Rory Byrne and his colleagues demonstrated to the FIA representative, Peter Wright, that the measurements taken in Sepang were not conclusive because the equipment used in Malaysia was not up to the job. This was the cornerstone of Ferrari's argument and the appeal judges in Paris agreed with it. Thus the Scuderia and Irvine were reinstated as winners and that meant there was everything to play for in the final race as they turned up at Suzuka leading both championships. The verdict was a complete vindication for Ferrari. Although the FIA seemed to have had its nose put out of joint, the president, Max Mosley, put a brave face on it.

Hakkinen, who had refused to celebrate when others thought he had the title in the bag, wisely choosing to await the outcome of the hearing, took the news philosophically, saying, 'I'm just thinking about the last race.'

The world championship would now be decided on the racetrack and not in court, which was great news for all race fans as Japan prepared to host the final round of the season. Schumacher did well in qualifying, taking pole position, but Irvine was back in fifth place, having destroyed his car when he hit the barrier. Ferrari was counting on Schumacher to stay out in front — a win could rob Hakkinen of the points he needed to take the title — but he made a bad start, just as he had done a year earlier when he was fighting for the title. Hakkinen led from the start and Schumi never got close. In the end, Irvine was running in third spot, but it was futile. Even if Schumacher let him through to second place, he would not have become champion. He would equal Hakkinen on points, but the Finn would take the title by virtue of having more wins to his name — five to Irvine's four. The curse of the final race had struck again. This was the third time in a row that Ferrari had lost the championship in the last 300 kilometres of the season.

Irvine took it well. 'We tried our best,' he said. Schumacher admitted to his mistake at the start, but conceded that 'the right driver won'.

That left the constructors' title — a consolation prize with a bitter taste although the team insisted it was important to them, due recognition for all their hard work. In fact, it was a marker, the first brick in the wall of a Ferrari revival, even if they did not know it yet. A trophy had not graced Maranello since the days of Tambay, Arnoux and Enzo Ferrari himself. Montezemolo attempted to talk up their achievement.

'For a team, the constructors' title is worth a great deal,' he said. 'This is the final championship of the century and Ferrari's name is back on the trophy for the first time since 1983. It is the first title for me as president, but I feel it will not be the last. We have the team, the men and the technology to have a great 2000.'

'Farewell until the next time' sounded like the usual rallying call of the past few seasons, but this time, the prophecy was entirely accurate. Ferrari's car and team were on the road to invincibility.

PREPARING TO TRAVEL TO MONZA

5

2000 – BOTH WORLD CHAMPIONSHIPS

The year of the red wigs

The 2000 season got off to an early start, just prior to the 1999 Italian Grand Prix, when Jean Todt invited Rubens Barrichello and his manager, Fred Della Noce, to dinner at his home in Maranello, the former country estate of a noble Modenese family. It was the ideal place to meet, far from the media spotlight that always shines on the world of Formula 1. The contract binding the Brazilian driver to Ferrari was signed that night.

Barrichello's name had made it on to the Ferrari wanted list back in 1995. Irvine got the job that time but in the space of four years, the Brazilian had matured, gained experience, dumped the unsuitable entourage who had followed him at every grand prix and employed the discreet, professional and competent Fred Della Noce as his manager. In short, he now had all the necessary qualities to wear the red suit with the Prancing Horse emblem on its heart, and he had the will to take on Schumacher's mantle one day. At twenty-seven, he already had seven seasons of Formula 1 behind him, spent with Jordan and Stewart. 'Young but experienced,' stressed the President. On top of that, he speaks excellent Italian, invaluable for dealing with Italian journalists and TV reporters. Thanks to a grandfather who originally came from Treviso, he even has an Italian passport tucked away in his back pocket, which would come in handy for zipping around countries in the European Union, whereas his Brazilian one would entail time-consuming visa requirements.

Over dinner, Barrichello talked about Ayrton Senna and the incredible bond that developed between them, and of the terrible pain that nearly broke him after 1 May 1994. The memory of that weekend is always with him, etched on Rubinho's heart. It all began with his dreadful accident at the Variante Bassa corner, when he was pitched into the catch fencing and rushed to hospital. He regained consciousness to find his friend Senna at his bedside. The next day, battered, bruised and bandaged, he returned to the track to show everyone he was up and about, before heading home to London. He did not get back in time to see Ratzenberger's fatal accident, but on Sunday he watched the scene that still sends shivers down the spine of anyone who sees it — the crash that claimed Senna's life.

It took Rubinho years to shake off the trauma of this experience, and also to cope with the pressure from Brazil, where the youngster was heralded as the heir to the late champion. Now, he was about to start again with Ferrari. The team that might well have welcomed Senna one day were giving him the chance to step up to the big time.

'Schumacher is a very strong driver, whom I respect, but I am not overwhelmed by him. All I ask is that I can play my cards in a healthy and correct fight on equal terms.' That was his only demand.

'Barrichello will not be Schumacher's water carrier. I put the same clause in his contract that is already in Schumacher's — the driver has to follow the orders and instructions of the Scuderia. There is no number one or number two driver. Ferrari's interests come ahead of those of the drivers,' explained Montezemolo, shortly before Christmas. Certainly Schumacher kept some clauses that gave him priority when it came to the availability of equipment, which, as usual for drivers of his status with most Formula 1 teams, had always been part of his contract with Maranello. A festive dinner with the Italian press is the traditional time for announcements and appraisals, and the President put a full stop to the 1999 season by presenting guests with a barge board off the F399. The joke, featuring the notorious Malaysian Grand Prix incident, was aimed at diffusing the tension of a season that was now done and dusted.

Before setting off again, there was some internal housekeeping to be done. These were minor changes only. The days of revolution were behind them. Luca Baldisserri, who had been Irvine's race engineer, was promoted to looking after Schumacher and his car. Ignazio Lunetta, who had worked with Schumacher since 1996, became the race team manager. Carlo Cantoni became Barrichello's race engineer, while Giorgio Ascanelli headed up research and development back at the factory. These small but significant changes were necessary to keep a mechanism that had begun to win going down the right road.

Every year since 1990, before the new car is unveiled, the Ferrari men have enjoyed a relaxing skiing week with the media in Madonna di Campiglio, organised by the Scuderia's title sponsor. On this occasion, Schumi skiied, played football, raced karts on ice and threw snowballs at Barrichello and Badoer, the broken leg a distant memory that didn't bother him any more. He was ready to take up the challenge again. Unsurprisingly, he admitted that he 'would like to become the first world champion of the new century. I have seen the mock-up of the new Ferrari. It looks very good and fills me with hope,' he smiled.

However, the rival teams were looking stronger than ever. Ferrari would be up against Mercedes with McLaren as before, but this year they would also have to face BMW with Williams, and Ford with Jaguar. Renault announced that as from 2001 they were buying the Benetton squad for $120 million and in 2002 an all-Toyota team were set to arrive on the scene. It was no longer a case of beating those whom Enzo Ferrari used to refer to as the 'English garagistes'. The opposition now consisted of true works teams, with a bigger annual budget than Ferrari and their sponsors could muster.

On 7 February, the F1−2000, the car with which Ferrari planned to defend the constructors' title and try to win the drivers' championship, was draped with a red sheet inside the Gestione Industriale building. President Montezemolo made a speech as usual but the unveiling ceremony was low-key. The only showy element was a film covering the story of championships won since 1961, plus a live video link to four departments of the factory — the foundry, the paint area, the engine assembly area and the production line. The point was to stress the importance of those who work at Maranello, each contributing to the winning of the constructors' championship, and to emphasise that Ferrari's philosophy in the twenty-first century remained centred on the factory and staff.

Schumacher declared his intentions when he said, 'I would really like to win the drivers' championship to bring the number 1 back to Maranello. The people who work here and the fans deserve it.'

Barrichello added his thoughts. 'I plan to take my first race win and maybe some more,' he said.

Ross Brawn delivered a typically British assessment of the triumphs of the previous year, including the verdict of the Paris tribunal, which overturned the sentence imposed by the Sepang stewards. And of course, the day would not have been complete without a prophecy from 'Avvocato' Agnelli, who never missed the baptism of a new Ferrari.

'It is the year of the reds,' he declared, 'a colour that seems equally popular in the world of politics.'

The new car may have had a rather banal code name in F1–2000 but there was nothing banal about its design. A more aggressive development with finer lines, considerably lower, than the car that had just won the constructors' title, it had a raised nose, which looked ready to sniff out victory. Most importantly, hidden away under the bodywork was the new 049 engine, with its V angle expanded from 80 to 90 degrees, offering a lower centre of gravity. It was under 600 millimetres in length and weighed close to 100 kilos, a little diamond set into the car.

All that remained was to hear the rumble of that engine and assess its driveability over the three kilometres of the Fiorano track. On the evening of 9 February, as dusk was falling, Schumacher got behind the wheel. It took him just a few laps to tell Todt and Montezemolo, 'That's it. The car is good.' Unfortunately, in this part of Italy the night air is bitingly cold and it affected his neck. The next day, he returned to the track at midday for the first real test but managed just six laps before his aching neck forced him to call a halt.

'Michael, it's better to stop and not risk making it worse,' advised his personal physio, who had looked after him for the past five years. Schumacher went along with the advice, not that he had a choice in the matter, irritation and disappointment written all over his face. He did not even stop to speak to RTL, the German TV station, also one of his sponsors, that pays for the privilege of always being the first to record his comments. His version of events came later in a short press release.

'It's a real shame I had to stop driving because the car felt really good and very sorted out. However, looking at the times for the few laps I did, I'm optimistic.'

He recorded a lap of 1 minute 01.26 seconds, which said a lot about the new F1–2000. Without doing any real set-up work, he had lapped within a second of the record that Luca Badoer had been so keen to set the previous week at the wheel of the old F399. Hence Schumacher's irritation at having to hand over the work to a beaming Barrichello.

The German's preparations had been scrupulous over the winter. He had even stayed in Dubai to train in the heat, so as to be in tip-top condition for the first winter test. On the day of the presentation, he looked so well that Jean Todt even commented on it, saying, 'I have never seen Michael looking so fit.' A silly stiff neck spoiled the plans.

Over the winter, prompted by Montezemolo, Michael had also begun to work on honing a more approachable image. In the months following his accident the previous year, he had found time to reflect on life in general. There had been too much gossip and misunderstanding, which only served to tarnish the reputation of a winning driver. It now seemed preferable to tidy up his relationship with the outside world and entrust it all to Ferrari. As part of this, Ferrari appointed Marlene, a student at Bologna University, to improve Michael's Italian, and on the day of the presentation he attempted to practise his new skills. Progress was noticeable but, ever the perfectionist, Schumi preferred to stick to either his native tongue or English, in which he is fluent, when it came to official engagements. However, in private, especially with the mechanics when they played football during test sessions, he would switch more and more frequently to Italian.

While Schumacher treated his aching neck, it fell to Barrichello to run in the new car. He went out on track in the afternoon and completed twenty-four laps, stopping the clocks in 1 minute 01.31 seconds, five-tenths of a second off Schumacher's time. These were good lap times, given that the car had done less than 100 kilometres.

'First impressions are very good,' confirmed Barrichello, without having had time to set his driving position exactly to his liking. The day's testing had been planned entirely around Schumacher. The next few days testing were also spent at Mugello, with Schumi back in the driving seat. There was just over a month left to prepare the F1−2000 for the start of the season, while their main rivals for the title had already been hard at work in Spain and England.

As has been the case since 1996, the first round took place in Melbourne. Schumacher had never won first time out with Ferrari although he had managed it twice with Benetton, both times in Brazil, in 1994 and 1995, the years when he took the title.

This time it was, yet again, an unexpectedly complicated start. During Friday's free practice, having set the fastest time, Schumacher crashed off the track into the barriers at 180 km/h at Turn 14, right in front of the grandstand that bears his name, crushing the left-side suspension. Jean Todt, ashen faced, watched as Schumacher clambered out of the cockpit unaided and waved to the crowd, indicating he was all right.

'I was just pushing too hard and went over the limit. The track was dirty and all it took was a little slide and I was off.' The memory of Silverstone and the accident in which he broke his leg the previous year was still fresh in his mind. 'I can't say I wasn't scared and didn't think of my accident. But this time the impact was on the side and not head-on, so it was not so bad. I don't know if this will have psychological repercussions, but for now, I feel fine, as if nothing had happened.'

In qualifying, the front row was an all McLaren-Mercedes affair, with Hakkinen and Coulthard the men to beat. The two Ferraris, with Schumacher quicker than Barrichello, were right behind on the second row. That is how the championship began, with Ferrari chasing McLaren and the titles — but after the first 307.574 racing kilometres of the year, Ferrari began to take flight. Schumacher won from Barrichello and that was the sign Maranello had been waiting for. It had been forty-seven years, back in the days of Ascari and Villoresi and the sport's romantic era, since Ferrari had kicked off with a one-two finish. The score was 16−0 in the fight with McLaren-Mercedes, as their rivals failed to get either car to the flag.

'I am happy, delighted in fact. We are now the quickest. I knew deep inside of me that we could do it and this Ferrari is too good not to be a winner. I was following Hakkinen and Coulthard, waiting for the pit stops to make a move. I realised that I could catch them and pass them.' Schumacher's official comments showed the team was on the right road.

Michael also admitted that during the closing stages of the race, he had talked to his car, saying such things as, 'Come on you beauty, come on and let's do it. Keep going, just another few laps and victory is ours.' Thus can develop a special relationship between man and machine – Schumacher and his Ferrari, almost a love affair.

Michael always speaks about his car with affection, admiration and gratitude. He talks of the car, the team and the men who support his efforts as family and he wants that world to work to perfection. So, having crossed the finish line in Melbourne, embraced his brother Ralf who finished third, sung the German anthem and conducted the Italian one from the podium, held the trophy aloft, sprayed the champagne and answered questions from a horde of journalists, he rushed to the garage to shake the hand of every single member of the team. Then the post-race celebrations made way for a ninety-minute debriefing, locked away with the engineers. His race was analysed corner by corner and all the computer data studied, linked in with the driver's view.

'We have a lot of ideas and we select, clarify and focus on the best ones. We have to look at the aerodynamics and the engine. We need to improve our start procedure and reduce fuel consumption,' he explained.

'Briefings with Michael are always productive and there is no risk of wasting time,' confirmed one of his engineers. 'He knows what we are aiming for and knows how to explain himself.'

The Schumacher show continued in Brazil and at Imola, making it three wins in a row, while Hakkinen picked up just six points thanks to second place in the San Marino Grand Prix. Coulthard was even further back with four points.

Reminding Schumacher that when a season starts in this fashion it usually ends up with a championship title is a risky business. It seems he is allergic to numbers and statistics. 'I'll study them when I'm a grandfather and I'll tell my grandchildren about them' is a favourite saying of his. They have the same effect on Montezemolo. He plunges his hands into his pockets to seek out a lucky charm, maybe a coral shell given to him by a fisherman in Capri. The fact remained that after such a convincing start, Ferrari could really think big. In 1976, Niki Lauda had his terrifying accident at the Nurburgring and the championship slipped from his grasp by just one point. That was the last year in which Ferrari won the opening two rounds of the season. Schumacher had now extended that winning streak to three.

In Brazil, an aggressive strategy, chosen along with Ross Brawn, once again helped his cause. He made it work with a great passing move on Hakkinen at the end of the pit straight. The only negative was Barrichello's retirement on lap twenty-eight with hydraulic problems. McLaren fared worse with Hakkinen's retirement followed by Coulthard's disqualification from second place. The end plates on the Scotsman's front wing were seven millimetres too low, two millimetres outside the permitted tolerance. The disqualification, confirmed at the appeal tribunal, was a real blow for Ron Dennis after the incident with the barge boards at the 1999 Malaysian Grand Prix. At that time, he had said, 'Dear Ferrari, the rules are the rules. If they are broken, even by just one millimetre, then that means disqualification.'

At Imola, Ferrari and Schumacher completed the hat trick and claimed another record. It was the first time in Ferrari's history that the same driver had managed to win the first three races of a season. The team had done it in 1976, but that year two drivers won — Lauda in Brazil and South Africa and Clay Regazzoni at Long Beach, USA. At Imola, Schumacher dominated and was once again helped by the team's choice of strategy, with the race transformed into a long series of qualifying laps. He got past Hakkinen after the second pit stop, coming in after the McLaren. This left Schumacher out on track alone to pull off an exploit summed up in his radio conversation with Brawn in those vital moments.

Then it was down to the pit crew, who were quick, precise and infallible. 'The best team won,' commented Schumacher afterwards, making it clear he felt this victory was not down to the car or driver, but to the whole team. He wanted to spread the praise to the 500 people working for him back in Maranello.

Montezemolo jumped in a helicopter in Bologna and in a very short time arrived at the circuit, where he embraced the entire team. Under the team awning, Fiat president Paolo Fresco was delighted, having watched the race with his wife Marlene. It was the first time he had experienced victory at first hand. The only person who needed consoling was Barrichello. A badly attached belt from his safety harness had given him cramps in his right thigh. 'Don't worry, Rubens. Your day will come soon,' prophesied the president.

Imola gave rise to controversy over Schumacher's start technique. 'It was a legal move, but definitely not a gentlemanly one,' said Norbert Haug, the Mercedes motorsport boss. He was commenting on the fact that, at the start, Schumacher had moved across the track, shutting the door on Coulthard. 'A racing move' was the stewards' verdict but in the pre-race driver briefings a rift began to grow between Schumacher and Coulthard, with Jacques Villeneuve and Eddie Irvine adding their criticisms. Sparks were flying, which was to be expected in view of the fact that Schumacher had scored thirty out of a possible thirty points.

The fourth grand prix of the season was scheduled to take place at Silverstone. Weather-wise, England at the end of April can be hellish. It began raining on the first day to such an extent that the organisers were forced to take the unprecedented step of issuing a statement: 'We would ask spectators to stay at home, as the car parks are flooded.' As for the track, it resembled a river. During Friday practice, the spray meant visibility was virtually zero. On Saturday, the situation improved slightly, and profiting from a brief ray of sunshine, Barrichello took his first pole position as a Ferrari man.

'As soon as I had done it, I felt butterflies in my stomach with the emotion of it all,' he said.

It was Ferrari's first pole position of the season, but so far in 2000, whoever had been quickest in qualifying had not gone on to win the race. The same thing happened at Silverstone. Barrichello took off in the lead and was going well, only to be sidelined by a failure in the hydraulic system.

Schumacher's race was spent swimming against the current. Starting from fifth on the grid, he found himself down in eighth after a tough fight with his brother at the first corner. In the end, third place could almost be considered a success, even if the two McLarens were ahead of him, Coulthard winning from

Hakkinen. The result sounded alarm bells in the Ferrari camp. The team still had a big lead in the championship, but it seemed the opposition had finally woken up.

McLaren's renaissance continued in Spain when it was Hakkinen's turn to win from Coulthard. A few days earlier, the Scotsman had walked away from a dramatic plane accident that had left the two pilots dead.

Schumacher was on pole in Barcelona but the race turned into a nightmare for Ferrari. During Schumacher's pit stop, the man operating the lollipop lifted it out of the way a fraction of a second too soon and as Schumacher pulled away, he ended up dragging chief mechanic Nigel Stepney along with him. Stepney was operating the refuelling hose, which was still locked on to the car. He was run over by a rear wheel and appeared to have twisted his ankle, but the following day, it transpired his right tibia was broken. The race continued and Schumacher's second pit stop also went wrong when the fuel line would not release from the car, losing him around ten seconds. In the space of two races, his championship lead had been slashed by half.

At the Nurburgring in the European Grand Prix, Schumacher was back on winning form. He got past Mika Hakkinen, this time on the track rather than in the pits, after the Finn had caught everyone napping at the start to lead from third on the grid. Ferrari had not won at the Nurburgring since 1985, when victory went to the unforgettable Michele Alboreto, and it was Schumacher's first win in Germany with Ferrari — two reasons to be even happier than usual. Schumacher was euphoric on the podium and after the champagne spraying, he explained the secret of his success.

'You want to know why I won? It's because of this,' he said, indicating a little violet brush. It was a present from his daughter Gina Maria. 'Take it Daddy, it will bring you luck,' the little girl had said, and the super champion, robot man, the best driver ever, had stuffed it in his pocket. Having won at home, the gift took on a special significance and became a symbol for the season.

For Ferrari, the little violet brush was not the only novelty at the Nurburgring. There was also a new refueller to replace the unfortunate Stepney on the rig. After a series of tests at Fiorano, the responsibility now fell to Pietro Timpini, a big lad well over six feet tall, and he handled five pit stops — two for Schumacher, three for Barrichello — without a single mistake.

'When Todt and Schumacher came to thank me and compliment me, it was really emotional,' said the man who from that day on has always been one of the two refuellers during pit stops.

Todt asked Luca Baldisserri, Schumacher's race engineer, to go up on the podium to collect the constructors' trophy.

'Todt took me by surprise. I was not expecting it. It was a big deal,' Baldisserri recalls. 'Beneath us, there was a huge sea of red caps, with the fans clapping, shouting and whistling. Michael was given his prize by the European Commissioner, Romano Prodi, and the German Chancellor, Gerhard Schroeder. Hearing the national anthem in this situation really gave me goose bumps and even the champagne tasted different — and it stings your eyes a lot.' Here was a happy man, blinded by the bubbles.

The only member of Ferrari to leave the Nurburgring down in the dumps was Rubens Barrichello.

'You should be happy with fourth place,' suggested Todt. Rubens was furious.

'This time we got it wrong,' he said, bluntly. 'It doesn't happen often at Ferrari, but the strategy was a disaster. I got the call for the first pit stop too late, just as I had gone past the pit-lane entrance. That extra lap on dry tyres cost me dear. To finish one lap down on the winner with a car that could have won is disappointing. I saw the ghosts of Imola again and I can't be happy with fourth place. Luckily, tomorrow is my birthday and I will celebrate without thinking about Formula 1.'

The root of Barrichello's problem and that extra lap on dry tyres was a misunderstanding with Ross Brawn. The slightest misunderstanding means the moment is lost and the whole race can change. These situations no longer arose with Schumacher but they were still a possibility for Barrichello in his first year.

'In the past few days, we have convinced him he has to talk more with the pits during a race. That way, these problems can be avoided,' commented Jean Todt.

Then it was on to Monaco and the weekend in the Principality turned out to be one of the most critical of the year for the red team. McLaren's big boss Ron Dennis declared, 'Ferrari is an elephant that we must eat one piece at a time.'

Schumi was sporting a new, all-red helmet design. His old helmet was too easily confused with Barrichello's, especially when seen in the tiny rear-view mirrors of a Formula 1 car. Now there could be no doubt about who was behind you, and in Monaco, ensuring that cars you are trying to pass can see and identify you is vital.

Nevertheless, Monaco 2000 was a black day for Ferrari. Schumi took pole and led for the first fifty-eight of seventy-eight laps, but then disaster struck as a left rear suspension arm broke due to a cracked exhaust pipe. With every lap, the exhaust pipe let out a rush of hot air, which had the same effect on the suspension as a blowtorch and the part finally failed.

The fault nearly put Barrichello out of the running too. After the finish, the mechanics discovered that the exhausts on his Ferrari were also split. It was a classic racing incident and Coulthard was quick to profit from it, going on to win from Barrichello and Fisichella. Thanks to those ten points, the Scotsman moved ahead of his team-mate Hakkinen in the championship — the Finn finished in sixth place — and was now Schumacher's closest rival, twelve points behind. Schumacher refused to be swayed, though, and still considered Hakkinen to be his most dangerous rival in the title fight.

However, in Montreal, having taken his third pole position of the season, Schumacher found Coulthard alongside him yet again on the front row, but the expected duel failed to materialise. As the cars prepared to leave the grid on the formation lap, three or four mechanics were still huddled round Coulthard's car, struggling to sort out a problem, and they failed to disconnect their laptops in time. As a result, the driver was given a stop-go penalty once the race was under way.

'I knew there was a problem with Coulthard's car because the pits told me, but I didn't bother about it, just running my race and making sure I didn't put too much strain on the brakes by pushing too hard while I still had a heavy fuel load. Around lap ten, I was told that Coulthard had a penalty and so I was able to ease off.'

Later, a red light on Schumacher's steering wheel display indicated a malfunction — overheating brakes to be precise. On lap forty-seven, he suddenly went off at the first corner and Ross Brawn radioed him to take it easy and not compromise the race. Further back, Barrichello had been asked to maintain station to protect his team-mate, which he did, coming home in second place.

'I could have won,' he commented after the race, 'if I had not been asked to slow down and if I had not lost time when my tyres were changed. But I'm not angry. I understand that Michael represents the present for Ferrari, while I could become its future.'

The parade-like finish in the rain brought Ferrari sixteen championship points, while Hakkinen had to make do with three from fourth place. Coulthard was seventh. It was something of a knock-out blow for McLaren. Going into the long European summer, Coulthard was twenty-two points down and Hakkinen twenty-four.

Schumacher was the first driver to have won from pole that season and he did not forget to give credit where it was due. 'I had Gina Maria's little violet brush with me,' he said.

The world title was now within reach but nothing can be taken for granted in Formula 1. This was the philosophy that Montezemolo and Todt had tried to inculcate within the team. Even when working hard, things can go wrong and for Schumacher they did, three times in a row. He failed to pick up a single point in France, Austria and Germany, while Hakkinen scored twenty-two and Coulthard twenty. The championship, which had seemed a foregone conclusion, was wide open again.

On top of the three races without points, Schumacher then endured another two without a win, in Hungary and Belgium, allowing Hakkinen, who took maximum points in Budapest and Spa, to move into the title lead with three races remaining. It was a complete turnaround.

In France, Coulthard won, having indulged in some theatrical over-reaction. After getting past Schumacher, he made a rude gesture in full view of the on-board TV camera, which beamed it around the world. The two had battled hard but it had been a fair fight and, once the race was over, David apologised to the TV viewers, especially young children. But the damage was done.

For Schumi, the day got off to a bad start with the mistake of choosing tyres that were too soft. It ended with a broken engine and retirement, and growing criticism of his actions at the start. He was accused of swerving across the track, closing the door too hard on whoever was alongside him. Race Director Charlie Whiting had to intervene, absolving the driver of any wrong doing. Starts were about to become a problem for Schumacher.

In Austria, the McLarens swapped positions, with Hakkinen coming home ahead of Coulthard, while Schumacher was out of action from the start, hit by Zonta after seven seconds, or 444 metres of racing. The race actually finished in the stewards room, as it was found that a seal was missing from the electronic control unit on car number 1, Mika Hakkinen's McLaren-Mercedes. The result was therefore in doubt for a few days, until the FIA decided that only the team would be punished, and the ten points they had scored would be deducted from the constructors' table.

A fortnight later in Germany, luckily for Ferrari and Schumacher, Barrichello limited the damage. From eighteenth on the grid, Rubinho took his first-ever win with a decisive and unusual strategy. This performance deprived Hakkinen and Coulthard, who finished behind him in that order, of some valuable points.

Schumacher suffered a repeat of what happened in Austria, hit at the start this time by Fisichella's Jordan, again after just seven seconds and around 400 metres into the race.

'It was like a truck on the motorway that suddenly brakes in front of you,' explained the Italian driver.

'Schumacher went that way only because ahead of him, Coulthard had closed the door, and when all's said and done, brakes are for braking,' countered Montezemolo.

At that point, it seemed Ferrari's race was over, with Barrichello languishing at the back of the pack, but a track invasion by a sacked Mercedes employee and a brilliantly planned and executed strategy turned the race on its head to deliver a great result. It is an achievement worth hearing first hand from those involved. By lap fourteen, Rubinho had already climbed back to fifth place.

Pits:	Rubens, get ready, pit stop in two laps.
Barrichello:	OK, I'm ready.
Pits:	Rubens, you're fifth, but you are now on level terms with the others. [All those ahead of him still had to make one stop.]

Rubinho continued to push, setting another fastest time on lap twenty, which would prove to be the fastest of the race, and closed on De La Rosa and Trulli. At this point, the spectator came on to the track and the safety car was called out.

Pits:	Rubens, safety car, pit immediately.
Barrichello:	OK, I'm coming in.

On lap twenty-five, Rubinho made his second stop, at the same time as Hakkinen. Coulthard was still out on track. When the Scotsman came in next time round, Rubinho found himself third, behind Hakkinen and Trulli.

Pits:	Rubens, you're third. Safety car still out. Don't overtake.
Barrichello:	OK.
Pits:	Rubinho, safety car coming in. Get ready for the restart. Don't overtake until you cross the line, don't overtake, remember.
Barrichello:	Understood.

The safety car came back out again after an accident involving Jean Alesi.

Pits:	Rubinho, be careful. Another safety car. Don't overtake, don't overtake.
Barrichello:	OK.

Around lap thirty-two, the race came to life.

Pits:	Rubinho, it's probably going to rain soon. We are ready with the wets when you want them.
Barrichello:	I'll wait.
Pits:	Rubens, it's raining. McLaren are getting ready to pit.
Barrichello:	It's not raining here, I'll keep going.
Pits:	Rubinho, Hakkinen's coming in, he's in. Trulli also. You're first! You can win. If you keep going like this, you can win!
Barrichello:	It's not raining on the straights. I can cope and I can hang on in the Motodrom. Give me the times, the times… How much am I losing out to Hakkinen?

A lap goes by.

Pits:	Listen Rubinho, if you keep up this pace, you've done it!
Barrichello:	I'll keep going, down the straight it's not raining, the chicanes are OK. It's not a problem for me.
Pits:	McLaren are ready again in the pits.
Barrichello:	I'll carry on. I can make it, I can make it.
Pits:	It's Coulthard.
Barrichello:	Where is Hakkinen?
Pits:	Ten seconds Rubinho, ten seconds. Six laps to go.
Barrichello:	OK.

From this point on, the pits give him only the gap time.

Pits:	9.5 seconds. Four laps.
Pits:	9.5 seconds. Three laps.
Pits:	12.2 seconds. Two laps. Concentrate Rubens, concentrate.
Pits:	11.5. It's the final lap. Take it easy, take it easy.

As Ferrari number 4 crosses the line, the mechanics get an earful in their headphones.

Barrichello:	Ooohooo, yessss, thanks, thanks to everyone.
Pits:	Well done, Rubens, that was great!

It was a performance that saved Schumacher's championship and rescued Ferrari from a summer-long crisis. With his first win from 123 races, the four points that Barrichello denied Hakkinen and Coulthard were enough to keep Schumacher in the lead of the championship, even after three consecutive retirements.

Nevertheless, Hakkinen's comeback continued with further wins in Hungary and Belgium. At the Hungaroring, Schumacher started from pole, but the Finn out-dragged him to the first corner and was never seen again. He also overtook Schumacher in the table, leading 64–62. Ferrari went straight back to work, even though it was a bank holiday. Engine, tyres, set-up and electronics were all studied and reworked at length. There were suspicions that one team was using a banned electronic differential, so Maranello fired off a letter to the FIA technical crew asking, 'Is it possible to use this type of differential?' The response was a definite no. Ferrari could not fit it to their cars. If someone was using it, it would have to be disconnected in a hurry to avoid disqualification.

In Spa, at the circuit where Schumacher made his Formula 1 debut in 1991 and took his first win in 1992, Hakkinen staged one of the most talked about overtaking moves in recent history. With three laps to go to the chequered flag, Schumi was about to pass Zonta in the BAR, but having chosen a wet set-up, the German was slower than his rival. He lined up the Ferrari on the Raidillon straight, moving to the outside with Zonta on his right — and Hakkinen shot through like a rocket to the right of the BAR, on the inside of the corner. It was a jaw-dropping manoeuvre and a dream pass, but it was not yet a pass to the championship. With four races to go, Hakkinen led his rival by just six points, 74–68.

Hakkinen's move was a heavy blow in championship terms but also for its effect on Schumacher's morale. With his back against the wall, Schumacher had to win again to reassert himself in a championship that earlier had seemed in the bag.

'This is a difficult moment,' said Gianni Agnelli at the Monza test session at the end of August, 'but it is in times of trouble that one discovers one's strengths and we have the men to do it. We believe in the championship and everyone in the team from Montezemolo down will tell you that, even if things go badly.' The message, delivered with affection, had an effect on the team. Above all, it brought stability to the squad, which had to deal with criticism after the Belgian Grand Prix.

When things are not going smoothly for Ferrari, the strangest hypotheses come to life — 'if they don't win the title, Schumacher will leave', 'if they don't win, Todt and Montezemolo will be chased out' and so on. Agnelli, honorary president and patriarch of Fiat, the biggest Ferrari shareholder, would have none of it. He intervened personally to ensure that peace and harmony reigned. It was just the right move to disperse the clouds of vitriol that were gathering and gave everyone in the team a morale-boosting injection of faith. The title was poised on a tightrope and the slightest error could mean that all was lost. This was the impetus for one last extraordinary push.

Schumacher did what had to be done in a time of crisis — he took pole position and went on to win the Italian Grand Prix, closing to within two points of Hakkinen, who finished second. In the media centre, immediately after celebrating the victory, Schumacher burst into tears. Never had he felt under so much pressure, so obliged to win. Also, he was touched because with that victory, the forty-first of his career, he had reached Ayrton Senna's record and because he had heard that a track marshal had been injured in an early race accident. His brother Ralf, alongside him on the podium and in the press conference, tried to console him.

'It's taken a weight off my shoulders,' said Michael. 'We have come through a difficult time when we were not as competitive as we should have been. First, I was knocked out on the first lap in two races, then I finished second in the next two, which I should have won. I had to win this weekend and I have done it in front of all these tifosi who have been supporting us. It is an incredible emotion and I cannot put the feeling into words.'

The team had moved closer to the target but the grand prix was a sad event. During the race, a wheel flew off Frentzen's Jordan, striking Paolo Ghislimberti, a young track marshal, at the second chicane. While Schumacher was shedding tears of relief, Ghislimberti lay in hospital, losing his fight for life. When he was told the news, Schumacher was in despair about what had happened to a young man who, like him, loved racing and cars. A few days later, back in communication with the outside world, he said, 'Unfortunately, racing is like that and the risk is ever present. In recent times, a lot has been done on the safety front, but we must not stop. We must continue to work on the cars and the circuits, for us drivers, for the people who work at the side of the track and for the spectators.'

From Monza, Formula 1 moved to the United States, which had not hosted a grand prix for the previous nine years. It was held at Indianapolis, making use of part of the legendary oval that was home to the Indy 500. The circuit was new to everyone, even Jacques Villeneuve, who had won there in 1995, and again Schumacher had the edge — it had happened in Malaysia a year earlier and it happened again in Indy.

'Michael needs just a handful of laps to learn a circuit and to push the car to the maximum,' explained Ross Brawn. Pole position and victory it said on the calling card he left for the Americans, who on this occasion at least, showed plenty of enthusiasm for Formula 1. The Ferrari one-two finish, with Schumacher ahead of Barrichello, was an amazing advertisement for the company — the United States is their biggest road-car market — but, at the time, Maranello was less concerned with selling cars and more interested in winning a title that had eluded them for too long.

The Indy race proved decisive. Schumacher took just a few hundred metres to get ahead of Coulthard at the first turn and led all the way to the flag. Coulthard, deemed to have jumped the start, was penalised ten seconds. Mika Hakkinen had had twelve consecutive points finishes, the last six also on the podium, but after twenty-five laps, he was forced to retire with a broken engine. That shot Schumacher into an eight-point lead in the championship, with just two races remaining. He had to finish second in both to become world champion.

Schumacher's only fright came with just five laps to go, twenty kilometres or so from the flag, when he spun off on to the grass.

'He called up the pits on the radio and said to stay calm. He was falling asleep and wanted us to keep talking to him so he didn't fall asleep again,' recounted Ross Brawn after the race. From then on, there was plenty of chat from the pits.

'I am in a strong position, it's true,' Schumacher told us, 'but I don't like celebrating in advance. I still have to get those two second places on the track.'

His words were nothing more than a façade. No one at Ferrari was thinking in terms of points or settling for second places.

'We have already started working hard on trying to win at Suzuka to finish things off properly,' Schumacher said later. 'Work, concentrate and work' is Schumacher's favourite method and the order of the day was to work as hard as possible, without overlooking the smallest detail. It involved checking the computer simulation and rechecking every part that was packaged and sent across the ocean, after making the most of every permissible kilometre of private testing.

Suzuka was not a place that held fond memories for the Scuderia. They had lost the last two drivers' world championships there, first with Schumacher and then with Irvine, and they had lost in 1990 with Prost, Ferrari's last attempt at the world championship prior to the Montezemolo era. More pertinently, Hakkinen had won the last two Japanese Grands Prix there, taking the title on both occasions. But in Italy, there is a saying 'never two without three', and Ferrari had already strung together three lost championships in 1997, 1998 and 1999 – 2000 was to be the turnaround year.

In Friday's free practice, which was affected by an earthquake tremor, Schumacher took pole ahead of Hakkinen by the tiniest of margins, just nine-thousandths of a second, or fifty-five millimetres. However, pole did not sit easily with him. He had been fastest in the two previous years and everyone remembered how those races ended.

Prior to this race, the international federation had stressed that any use of blatant team orders would be punished. They even rustled up a new black and white flag to indicate the infringement but there was no need for it this time. Once again, Michael made a poor start, his Ferrari slewing almost sideways while Hakkinen shot off to lead going into the first corner. From then on, it turned into a duel between the two of them.

'I got too much wheelspin and I tried to keep Hakkinen behind me by moving to the right,' Schumacher explained later, 'but he made a very good start and took the lead. At that moment, I realised it would all be decided during the pit stops.'

Tactics therefore came into play, coordinated by Ross Brawn — 'a masterstroke' according to Schumi. The ploy consisted of delaying Schumacher's second stop, leaving him out on track for three laps longer than his rival, which was enough for him to rejoin the track in the lead. This strategy had to be planned in advance because it affected the amount of fuel taken on at the first stop.

'We calculated how much fuel to put in Michael's tank to allow him to stay out longer than Hakkinen,' said Ross. 'We knew the McLaren would have to stop around lap thirty-seven, based on what they did last year and in their first stop. When Mika came in on lap thirty-seven, I told Michael to go flat out, to do one, two, three qualifying laps in a row. He was perfect, as was the team because the second stop was very quick. Michael rejoined in the lead with thirteen laps to go. The job was done.'

The few seconds it took Michael to move down the pit lane in order to get back on track, with the speed limiter set at the regulation 80 km/h, seemed like an eternity. Ross Brawn had one eye glued to the TV monitor and the other on the track, straining for sight of the McLaren. The closer Schumi got to the pit-lane exit, the more optimistic became Ross's cries over the radio.

Brawn: Come in Michael, hot stop, come in, hot stop.

OK Michael, he's going to be there, when you get out he's going to be there. I'll try to talk you through it. You're looking good, it's looking good, it's looking good... It's looking fantastic, Michael, well done, well done! P1, P1, fantastic! Just keep it on the road now.

With less than eighty kilometres to go, the moment of triumph was approaching. At the finish, the whole Ferrari team erupted. Back home in Bologna, Montezemolo's phone rang. Only one man was allowed to ring him at times like these — 'Avvocato' Agnelli. 'It's done, Luca. Stay calm. It's done now,' he said. Those who know Montezemolo understand that the last moments of a race are the worst for him. Even though this time it was a sweet finale, 'I got emotional and cried,' he admitted later.

Once across the finish line, Schumacher howled with joy down the microphone inside his helmet. Later he said that during those last thirteen laps, he had been 'thinking of the man above who guides us all. I am a believer. Maybe no one knows this but after every race, win or lose, I thank God.' He punched the air and almost came to a stop. He had just made history and was incapable of getting out of his car. He sat there motionless for a few seconds, paralysed with the emotion of it all, crippled with happiness. He punched the air again, grabbing at the rain. Finally, he got out of the cockpit and took off his helmet and fireproof balaclava. His eyes were damp and he had the same expression as in Monza when that weight was lifted from his shoulders. He hugged Barrichello, he hugged Todt, the only team member allowed near him, leaning on his shoulder and shedding a tear or two. He shook hands with Hakkinen, his most respected opponent, and with Coulthard, of whom the same could not be said. Then he ran to the fence and hugged all his mechanics, his engineers and Corinna, pulling her to him and giving her a long lingering kiss on the lips.

On the podium, he did his highest ever victory leap before standing for the German and Italian national anthems. He hugged Todt, who held him hard and lifted him in the air. After twenty-one years, 7,700 days and an investment of $3,500 million, Ferrari had won the drivers' title again — from Jody Scheckter to Michael Schumacher, from Enzo Ferrari to Luca di Montezemolo.

'After this success our professional life will never be the same again,' said Todt to Michael.

'This is my third world championship, but it is a special one, the best and the most emotional. It is five years since I was last champion and I did not expect to wait so long, but I always believed we would do it. This is the greatest moment of my career, the best moment. Winning with Ferrari feels special and has a special significance as Ferrari is Formula 1,' said Schumacher, trying to explain his innermost feelings.

A congratulatory fax arrived from the German Chancellor, Gerhard Schroeder, while Agnelli and Montezemolo reached for the phone. The TV showed images of celebration in Italy and in Michael's home-town of Kerpen. The result brought Schumi overwhelming joy and he wanted to hang on to it all. The title was for him. He had no intention of dedicating it to anyone special, not even to Gina Maria, who had given him a special good-luck charm for the occasion in the shape of a little blue bell, part of a toy alarm-clock.

But the Ferrari family has a habit of finding the time and the level-headed desire to think about the future, even in the middle of a celebration.

'For now, let me enjoy this title, but I can assure you that I have other ambitions to pursue with this fantastic team. Even Mika did not stop thinking about winning after he took his first title. I have definitely not had enough. I want to win some more with this team,' insisted the world champion.

'This is a victory for Italian technology. Ferrari does everything in-house, even if in the team we have French, English, Canadians, South Africans and Germans. We have won in Japan, the land of hi-tech. We have extended the legend. Enzo Ferrari would be proud of us and of this Ferrari team,' added President Montezemolo, while Italy celebrated as if it had won the World Cup.

In order to complete the celebrations, one more achievement remained — the constructors' championship. McLaren was thirteen points behind and, mathematically, still in with a chance. The championship drew to a close on 22 October with the Malaysian Grand Prix and anyone who expected to find Ferrari still in party mood was in for a surprise.

'We are only at the start of a string of victories,' warned Todt, and he was right. In Malaysia, Schumacher continued his winning run with a fourth consecutive pole and a fourth consecutive victory, significant for Ferrari because it was the tenth win of the season, which added up to 170 points scored and the constructors' title.

So it was full house and the party could kick off again. Out of the packing cases that carry the spare parts came dozens of red wigs. Ross Brawn, Barrichello and Schumacher donned them on the podium. Then, one by one, every single mechanic turned into a redhead, a Ferrari-redhead. Montezemolo arrived and even he put on the victory wig.

'I've got butterflies in my stomach with the excitement of it all,' said Schumacher with an unusually good grasp of English expressions.

It had been a perfect year. It seemed logical to say it was unrepeatable, but when you are dealing with Ferrari and Schumacher, it is dangerous to stick to logic. Soon it became clear that this was just the beginning. A new era was dawning, a Ferrari era, the longest and most convincing domination by a single team in the entire history of Formula 1.

ITALIAN GRAND PRIX 2003, MONZA

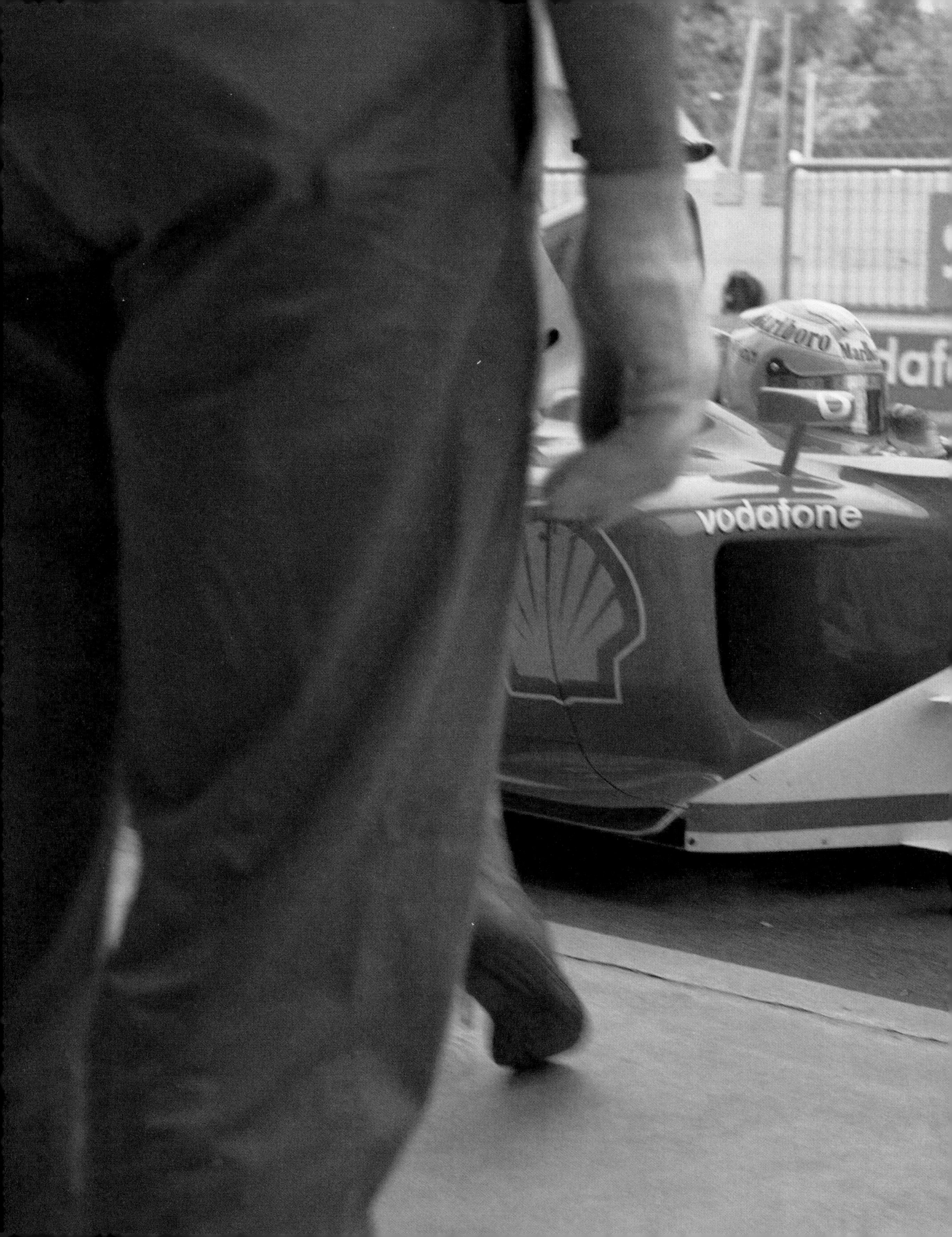
vodafone

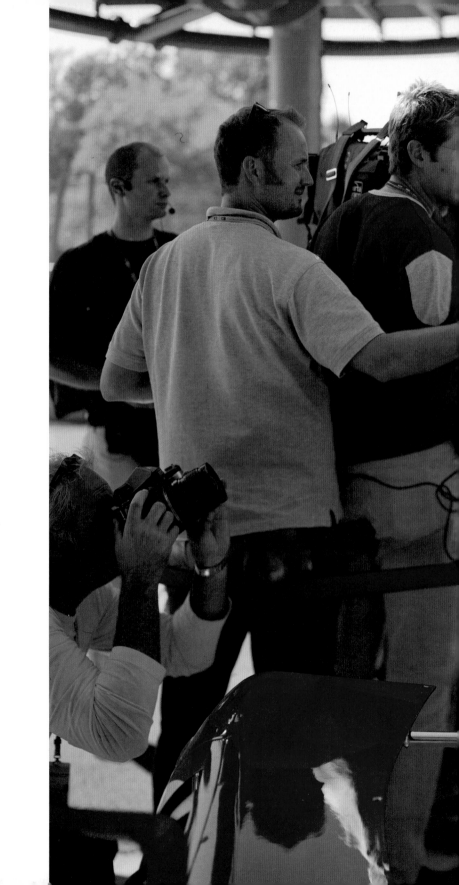

6

2001 – THE CONFIRMATION

Winning is always more difficult second time around

In sport, there is only one thing harder than winning and that's doing it a second time. 'Winning again' was a phrase that began to be bandied about at Ferrari as soon as the Sepang party to celebrate both 2000 world championship titles was over. It was a phrase that would be repeated several times in the first three years of the new century.

However, at the start of 2001 it seemed impossible to improve on the results of the previous year. What more could be wished for than ten wins and two world titles? Easy – winning the championship with a few races in hand. That was the target for the men in red. 'What are we lacking in order to win again? Nothing,' according to President Montezemolo on Monday, 29 January, the day the new car, the F2001 was unveiled. This was the first Ferrari Formula 1 car in twenty-one years that could set off without the weight of the world on its shoulders. The number 1 it bore on its red livery had been won on the track, unlike the ones that Alain Prost brought with him in 1990 and Michael Schumacher carried over in 1996.

'The title must stay with us,' declared Michael. You only had to see the smile on his face as he pulled the wraps off the new F2001 to know that his enthusiasm had not diminished one jot. He looked ecstatic, happier even than Rubens Barrichello and Luca Badoer, who helped him unveil the Miss World Ferrari.

'Good morning, everyone. I don't want to say too much as our two world championship titles say it all. Winning with Ferrari is something special. I want Ferrari to stay number one for many years to come and that is what we are fighting for. Forza Ferrari,' said Michael in Italian. It was evident that the world champion was as motivated as ever and no less combative than before. 'I can't wait to get in the new car and fire it up. I like this car. At first glance, it looks similar to last year's, but a closer look shows it has a lot of new elements. It seems a bit bigger than the F1–2000, but it will be more comfortable and safer. With a car like this, I would not have hurt myself at Silverstone.'

On Thursday, 1 February, the new F2001 was tested at Fiorano, its debut producing a record lap and going off without a hitch. It covered over 200 trouble-free kilometres and set a time of 59.505 seconds, a record for a car on grooved tyres. The performance spoke volumes about the potential of the latest creation to emerge from Maranello. 'This is the right Ferrari to win again,' commented Schumacher.

Schumacher knows how to channel the work of the engineers and mechanics, as Ross Brawn explained. 'We have never built a car specifically for Michael. When we start working on a new car, we just try to improve over the previous year's machine. Certainly, the relationship we now have with him means that we can ask whether or not he feels something is worth trying,' said Brawn.

One week after the new car launch, Jean Todt, Ross Brawn and Rory Byrne signed new contracts, extending their stay at Maranello to the end of 2004. Eventually, they would agree to stay even longer.

The championship got under way in Australia, and Ferrari turned up in Melbourne without having completed a race distance in testing. This was also the case with the new McLaren-Mercedes. Both teams would have preferred a few more weeks to shake down their new cars but come 4 March it was time to go racing again and, as it turned out, to continue their duel for the fourth year, with the other teams relegated to the role of also-rans. An interesting new actor stepped on to the Formula 1 stage in the shape of Colombia's Juan Pablo Montoya, CART champion and winner of the previous year's Indy 500. He would be a rival for the future, but for the time being, Hakkinen was still the main opposition, even though Mika soon realised he had had enough of racing.

It is not Schumacher's style to brag and so when he claimed to be 'as strong and fit as Rambo' he meant it. 'I met Sylvester Stallone in New York, where we went to the gym together. Purely in terms of the weights, I was not lifting any less than he did,' Michael remarked, but his muscles were not much use come Friday morning and the first practice session for the Australian Grand Prix, when he had a falling out with his Ferrari. He went off the track at 180 km/h at turn six and flipped over twice. For those watching, it was a frightening sight. Corinna, who was waiting for him back in the pits to celebrate her birthday, went pale. But Michael stepped out of the car unscathed, even having his photo taken with an eighteen-month-old baby in a red romper suit.

'The accident looked very spectacular from outside the car,' Michael explained, 'but from inside the car, it was nothing special. I was expecting a much heavier impact, but by the time the car landed back on its wheels, most of the energy had been absorbed. I'm perfectly fine and don't have a scratch. My only concern is for the car. I hope the mechanics can get it back. It's proving to be very quick, lovely.'

He was not exaggerating. He took pole position and went on to win the race and give Ferrari yet another victorious debut. But celebrations were muted because, in a similar scenario to the one that cost the life of Paolo Ghislimberti at Monza the previous September, a marshal died after being hit by a wheel. The tragedy occurred after Villeneuve and Ralf Schumacher collided. The Canadian's BAR flew through the air and a wheel struck the Australian marshal at the side of the track, while flying debris left nine spectators with slight injuries. Villeneuve stepped out of the cockpit shaken but unhurt. It was a sad end to the afternoon and the world of Formula 1 had to ask itself why, in the space of just a few months from September to March, two marshals had been killed at the side of the track, where they worked for love not money. These days, the drivers are well protected, as was seen when Hakkinen had an accident, flying off the track at 305 km/h after his suspension broke. The mechanics are also protected, but not those who work on the fringes of the Formula 1 circus so that the heroes of speed can continue to do battle.

'We have won just one race out of seventeen,' said Todt. 'The work we have done so far has paid off and all we can do is continue in the same way, by working more.' His words rang out like a call to arms. This was no time for resting on laurels. A fortnight later in Malaysia, Schumacher notched up another win, this time rounded off with a second place for Barrichello to give the Scuderia its fiftieth one-two finish. For Schumi, it was his sixth consecutive win, taking into account the last four races of 2000. However, Barrichello's nose was out of joint and he said as much in a live TV interview.

'Michael should not have overtaken me like that. His passing move was a sad thing to happen,' said Rubens. He was alluding to what happened on lap twelve after the safety car had returned to the pits. 'I had only just said to Ross on the radio that we had to be careful when the race got under way again because there were still puddles on some parts of the track. I wanted to make up ground, but I got too close to the Jordan in front of me. I lost momentum and Michael passed me. In this sort of situation, a team-mate should have maintained position and not done this,' Rubinho continued in the official press conference, with a shocked looking Schumacher sitting alongside him.

'I don't think it's important what Ross said to me on the radio,' came Schumi's response. 'Rubens can look in the mirrors and see what's about to happen. We were on equal terms and fighting for position. I don't think I did anything wrong.'

It took a while for Barrichello to realise he had said too much and may have exaggerated a bit. Leaving aside the comments of the two drivers made in the heat of the moment, the incident was due to a misunderstanding. Rubens was not expecting his team-mate to try to pass him at that moment, while Michael felt he could. All that mattered to Ferrari was that they had taken two wins from two races and the championship had got off to the best possible start.

'At the start of the season, there are no team orders between our drivers. Rubens should have expected the move from Michael. His outburst was just a moment of emotion. We have spoken about it and explained everything,' clarified Jean Todt. Other moments of friction and tension arose over the year, with team orders coming into play, but fortunately, one of Ferrari's strengths is that working relationships within the team are solid enough to withstand these situations, which have no lasting effect.

'What Rubens said in Malaysia will not affect our relationship. He is still my strongest rival,' said Schumacher when he arrived in Sao Paolo for the third race of the year, putting a conclusive stop to all the gossip. This was Barrichello's home race, held just a stone's throw from the apartment where Rubens was brought up, but Michael had the last word. 'Let him win in front of his home crowd? Why? We are fighting for the championship and this is not the time to give out presents.' Team-mates yes, friends even, but the world championship was another matter.

Schumacher took his seventh consecutive pole position, fighting off a family member in the process — not Barrichello this time, but his brother Ralf. In fifty years of Formula 1, two brothers had never before shared the front row of the grid. It finally happened on 31 March 2001, although it took a while to be confirmed while a lengthy analysis was carried out on the fuel used in Ralf's Williams-BMW.

'We will be calm and there will be no disasters,' promised the two prior to the start, but a third player threw his hat in the ring — David Coulthard. The Scotsman was McLaren-Mercedes' sole driver after Hakkinen was left stranded on the grid with an engine problem, and he went on to win the race. Michael came home second, struggling with set-up problems. Unfortunately, Barrichello put himself out of the running, colliding with Ralf's Williams.

It was not a good Sunday for Schumi. In the dry, he was passed by Montoya, and in the wet, Coulthard did the same. Both moves happened at virtually the same place, the end of the main straight as the track dives down to the left. Montoya caught Schumi napping when the safety car pulled in on lap three, but on lap thirty-nine, he was calamitously crashed into by Verstappen. As for Coulthard, he surprised Schumacher when it began to rain. Wet conditions normally signify victory for the German, but not this time. He even spun off the track. Without the right set-up to push on in the wet, Michael had to admit defeat. His run of six consecutive wins had come to an end and Coulthard was now his main rival for the title, just six points behind. Hakkinen was languishing on a single point, picked up courtesy of sixth place in Australia.

'Stay calm, Ferrari will be back on winning form in Imola,' was Schumacher's response, but this time his powers of prediction let him down. He was already off the pace in qualifying fourth and he was knocked out of the race when, after being slowed at the start with a gear-change problem, a damaged left rear wheel caused a puncture. But a Schumacher did win — Ralf. Michael was happy enough.

'He deserves this win, which has been a long time coming,' Michael said. 'He would have done it sooner but for some bad luck. Mum and Dad will be proud of us and so will our manager.'

Nine years after Michael, Ralf took his maiden victory. Two brothers had never won grands prix before. It was the only thing that put a smile on Michael's face, as Coulthard had now joined him at the head of the championship table. Ferrari's only points from this home race were those that came with Barrichello's third place. Rubinho drove a very consistent race with a risky strategy of making a very late first stop, having started from sixth on the grid. At least he made it to the podium.

Before flying off to Barcelona for the Spanish Grand Prix, Ferrari joined others in mourning the loss of one of their former drivers, the very popular Michele Alboreto, the last Italian to win a grand prix at the wheel of a red car. Alboreto died on 24 April after an accident at the Lausitzring, where he was testing an Audi R8 in preparation for the Le Mans 24 Hours.

A tyre blow out caused the car to take off and for Michele there was no escape. He would have turned forty-five in December, and he left a wife, Nadia, and two small children. His death left a great void for those who knew him well. Michele was one of the last drivers to have been taken on by Enzo Ferrari and a great favourite with the Old Man. He drove eighty races for Ferrari out of a total of 194 grands prix, winning three for the Scuderia, five in total, and in 1985 he was a title contender with Alain Prost. The world of Formula 1 paid tribute but the work went on, just as he would have wished.

Spain staged the fifth round of the championship, and extensive use of electronic driver aids was once again made legal. One of these gizmos let Coulthard down, leaving his McLaren stranded on the grid on the formation lap, and as a result, instead of starting third behind Schumacher and Hakkinen, he had to start from the back. The race thus turned into a duel between the two old adversaries, Schumi and Hakkinen. They had been fighting for the title for the past four years, with mutual respect characterising their battles. It had proved virtually impossible to get one of them to say a bad word about the other. Michael had always rated Mika as one of his most gentlemanly opponents and during test sessions they would often stop in the pits to compare notes about their children. Not the best of friends, they were certainly more than just acquaintances.

This relationship was the reason Michael did not gloat over events that afternoon of 29 April in Barcelona. Hakkinen moved into the lead after Schumacher's second pit stop and was still there right up to the last lap coming up to turn five. In the pits, two famous guests of Ron Dennis, Catherine Zeta Jones and husband Michael Douglas, were ready to pop open the champagne when Mika was let down by his clutch. The engine on his McLaren died and victory was snatched from him. Schumacher was handed the win on a plate, along with ten very important points in the championship. At the finish, he hugged Hakkinen, almost apologetically.

'It was a shock to see him out of the race like that. I really feel sorry for him and it's not nice winning in this way. It's not the best way to win, passing a car at the side of the track. I am very sorry, but in racing these things happen and they have happened to me in the past. Remember with the Benetton in Monaco, I lost a race I thought was in the bag. But losing a race on the last lap, no, that's never happened to me. It must be terrible. I can only imagine what Mika must have felt.' He was genuinely upset and did not perform his customary victory leap on the podium nor did he conduct his mechanics in singing the Italian anthem. 'We had a great fight for fifty laps. Sometimes he was quicker and other times it was me. We had fun, really pushing like mad, but in the end, Mika deserved the win. I'm sorry, really sorry, especially as he is going through a difficult time right now and a win would have done him good.'

However, not wishing to look a gift horse in the mouth, Michael eventually dedicated the win to Montezemolo and his wife Ludovica, who had just had a baby girl, Guia. At the end of the day, ten points were ten points however they were obtained, and with them, Schumacher extended his lead over Coulthard, who was fifth in the race. Alongside him on the podium were the new boy Montoya, making his first visit, and an old hand in the form of Villeneuve, who had been out of championship contention for some time since joining BAR in 1999. After five races, Michael was in control of the championship.

Then came Austria, one of the few circuits where Schumacher had never managed to win. Everything seemed to go well in qualifying, very well in fact. Schumacher took his thirty-seventh pole position, followed by the two Williams-BMWs and Barrichello. Championship rivals McLaren-Mercedes tied themselves in knots over set-up and were further back, with Coulthard seventh and Hakkinen eighth.

Things got complicated right from the start. Four cars were stuck on the grid — Hakkinen, Trulli, Heidfeld and Frentzen. Schumacher at least managed to get off the line, although not brilliantly. At the first corner, he was third behind the charging Montoya and Schumacher the younger. Ralf retired after ten laps and the gap between Michael and Montoya grew smaller, Schumacher closing right up and trying to get by once, twice, three times, but to no avail. On lap sixteen, he gave it his all. At the hairpin, he attacked round the outside, but Montoya would not give way, braking very late and forcing both cars to run wide with the Ferrari ending up in the gravel. Barrichello said thanks and whizzed by both cars to take the lead.

Schumi and Montoya rejoined in sixth and seventh places respectively. Rubinho kept the lead until lap forty-seven when he came in for his pit stop. Coulthard had been right behind him and waited a further three laps before making his stop, from which he emerged in front. It was game over. Coulthard flew to the chequered flag ahead of Barrichello, who had now been caught by Schumacher. At this point, Jean Todt and Ross Brawn decided to ask Barrichello to make the sacrifice and let Schumacher pass to invert their positions behind Coulthard. The difference between second and third places is two points and second place would allow Schumacher to maintain a four-point advantage over Coulthard, whereas third place would drop him to just two points clear. The reasoning was purely mathematical.

'Rubens, let Michael pass… Rubens, let Michael pass for the championship… Let him pass, please…'

Rubinho thought about it before doing as he was asked. He waited until he was just a few hundred metres from the finish line before lifting off the throttle, which made it fairly obvious he was acting under instructions.

'I never doubted Rubens' professionalism,' insisted Jean Todt.

'The team asked me to do it. They asked me several times, but that's not what bothers me. Rather, it's the overall situation in the race. I could have won. I didn't because Coulthard got past by staying out on track four laps longer than me, while I was on the limit with my fuel and I had no alternative but to pit.' Rubinho looked sad while he delivered his thoughts. He had the look of someone who had found obeying orders hard to swallow. A little later, he tried to lighten the mood with a quip — 'I hope that, come the end of the season, I don't lose the championship by two points.'

Naturally, Ferrari's instructions provoked a major storm of controversy. Rivals had been waiting for something to latch on to and now they had something to criticise. Predictably, Schumacher sprung to the team's defence.

'And if we had not done it? And then lost the title by two points? No, Ferrari's philosophy is clear — we defend the driver who is best placed in the championship. I don't think you can talk about unsporting behaviour. There is nothing in the rules to say you can't do it,' he said.

The incident was a foretaste of what would happen a year later, again in Austria, when Rubens was forced to move over again, this time to let Michael take the win.

In the days following the Austrian race some important decisions were made. First Montezemolo, who had been invited by Silvio Berlusconi to join the Italian government, said thank you but chose to stay with Ferrari. Then, in the space of a few days, news broke that Schumacher had extended his contract to the end of 2004 to coincide with those of Todt, Brawn and Byrne, and Barrichello had extended his to the end of 2002. Even after Austria, the two drivers, who might have appeared to be going through a crisis, were passionate about sticking together. It was a sign of stability, one of the secrets of 'Formula Ferrari'.

'For me, Ferrari is a second family,' commented Schumi.

That stability characterises Montezemolo's Ferrari. In the years before he took control, even in the first years of his reign, the Ferrari offices were like the lobby of a hotel, with constant coming and going, but in the last few years there has been minimum interference with the basic structure of the team. A few little touches have been apparent here and there, the odd moving around of personnel and some new blood, but not in the key positions. Everyone works together towards the common goal.

'It was not difficult to convince Michael. He has understood what it means to drive for Ferrari and to win for Ferrari. One championship with us is worth more than two with anyone else,' explained Montezemolo.

In Monaco, Schumacher was back to his winning ways, despite the fact that pole position went to local resident David Coulthard. Once again the McLaren was left stranded on the grid for the formation lap and David went from first row to last. Every one of the seventy-eight laps at this circuit can catch you out with hidden dangers. A moment's inattention can result in a car ending up in the barriers, leaving it with bent suspension and the driver with a long walk back to the pits. Schumacher kept his concentration by chatting. Lap after lap, he bombarded Ross Brawn with questions — 'What happened to David? Where's Mika? What happened to my brother?' — just to see the big picture.

'Actually, the only danger is getting bored on the track,' Schumacher said afterwards. 'It's not easy to stay concentrated for the whole race. It was a dull grand prix without any real fights. From before the start right to the finish all sorts of things go through your mind and you have the strangest thoughts about what could complicate your life before the finish, especially after what happened to me here last year when the exhaust broke.'

Fortunately, everything went well. Barrichello gave the team another one-two finish, while former team-mate Eddie Irvine completed the podium trio in his Jaguar.

'This time I was calm,' explained Schumi. 'I had a secret weapon. This morning, Corinna found a four-leaf clover, which she gave to me.'

The tables turned again in Canada. Schumi was back on pole, just ahead of Ralf, but the race did not go his way. The Williams tank had more fuel on board than the Ferrari and that was all it took to make the difference. Ralf pitted five laps later than Michael and it proved to be the winning tactic.

'We are really a happy family,' they said as one.

'It's lucky there's only two of them,' joked Hakkinen, who shared the podium with them.

'I prefer a win for Ralf rather than anyone else,' added Michael. 'I've picked up some valuable points and he's taken his second win. It's the first time we've finished first and second, which is reason to be happy.'

The Ferrari man now had an eighteen-point lead over Coulthard, who was sidelined with a broken engine. This underlined another of the Scuderia's strengths in the fight against Coulthard, the main rival for title honours — its reliability.

The happy family did not stay that way for long. The European Grand Prix at the Nurburgring provided the setting for a fratricidal fight. Before the start, Michael went through one of the strangest moments of the season. Luckily, it was before the start and not a few metres after it. His Ferrari, which was in fact the spare car, died on him as he drove round to take up pole position on the grid. He just managed to park it off the track, commandeer a politically incorrect BMW C1 scooter and rush back to the pits to jump into the other car in time to line up on the grid, ahead of Ralf.

When the red lights went out, the Williams-BMW was fastest away, but Michael was having none of it. He changed his line slightly, heading for the inside, and managed to fend off his brother. The move was hard but fair.

'I would not have put him into the wall,' he maintained later. Ralf did not take it well.

'You should not do that to me,' he replied.

Ralf tripped himself up coming out of the pits after his stop on lap twenty-eight when he straddled the white line marking the end of the pit lane and was given a stop-go penalty. He had been catching Michael but this effectively put him out of the hunt.

'The rules have to be obeyed,' was Michael's comment to Ralf. 'It's happened to me in the past, being penalised for a minor infringement.'

Schumacher arrived in France with a twenty-four point lead over Coulthard, with everyone working out the figures to see when, rather than if, he would become world champion. However, pole position went to Ralf. Their spat at the Nurburgring had been resolved but Ralf was becoming a serious rival. 'And this time, I will do everything I can to stay in front,' was his ironic comment.

The start went off smoothly for all but Hakkinen, who yet again found himself stranded on the grid with a gearbox problem on his McLaren. Once more, the deciding factor between the Schumacher brothers was race strategy and pit work. Michael stayed out on track one lap longer than Ralf and that was enough for him to get ahead and disappear into the distance, claiming 'a perfect victory'. It was the fiftieth of his career, his brother and his team-mate were on the podium with him, and championship rival Coulthard was way back, delayed by a penalty for speeding in the pit lane. 'After the pit stop, my Ferrari was flying. It is incredible to drive a car like this,' Michael said, hardly able to contain his euphoria.

The world championship was now well and truly within his grasp, as he had a thirty-one point lead over Coulthard. 'But with seven races still to go and seventy points up for grabs, I prefer not to lose my concentration. Hakkinen has picked up nine points from the last ten races and if the same thing happened to me, I could say bye-bye to the world championship. No, I prefer to think of the championship race by race, not to plan anything, not to organise any celebrations too soon.'

Schumacher was being realistic, refusing to get carried away and keeping his emotions under control. No one in the squad was about to lose touch with reality, which was another example of Ferrari's strength. Win or lose, the follow-up was always the same — work, work and more work.

However, prior to the British Grand Prix on 14 July, there was time to celebrate an historic anniversary. It was fifty years since the team's first Formula 1 victory, won at Silverstone in 1951 by José Froilan 'Cabezon' Gonzalez. On Sunday morning, before the race, Schumacher drove a lap of the track in a car from the fifties, the 375 F1 giving him an inkling of what racing was like in the early days. It also prompted further comparisons with Fangio, which were becoming ever more common.

Schumacher started the race from pole — for the first time at this track — which kept him out of trouble when Trulli and Coulthard tangled at the first corner, but he could not make a break. Hakkinen hung on and, on lap five, passed the Ferrari at Copse. Montoya was charging through the field from eighth on the grid and he too got past, on lap eighteen. Ferrari's strategy, based on a single stop, was not the right one this time, even though Michael at least made it to the podium. After fourteen races and 322 barren days, Hakkinen tasted victory once more and Schumacher was happy all the same.

'My car was not well balanced,' he said. 'In some parts, it was oversteering and in others it wasn't. We had not had time to try the new tyres and my main concern was keeping the car on track. So when Mika attacked, I didn't try to fight back. I knew Coulthard was already out of the race. I didn't jump for joy but simply concentrated on being careful, thinking of the points advantage and looking after it.'

The six points he took for second place increased his lead over Coulthard in the title chase. The gap was now thirty-seven points, which meant that Schumacher could become world champion if he finished no better than third in the remaining six races with Coulthard winning all of them. 'This result was as good as a soccer team securing a draw in an away game,' commented the men in red.

'On a few occasions, I've had a drop in concentration and I can assure you it's not a nice feeling,' Schumacher explained. 'But this time, it was just the way the race went. My best time was half a second slower than Mika's, so it was pointless to take any risks. We realised that the McLarens were very quick here. It's their home track, but I'm not saying that to suggest it gave them an advantage. I will continue to fight for victory right to the very end of the championship, but if I find myself in a similar situation again, I would do the same.'

But, as has been said many times, in Formula 1 nothing can be taken for granted. Danger lurks around every corner. Michael Schumacher learnt that to his cost on Tuesday, 17 July at Monza in a testing session when he crashed into the barriers at 315 km/h at the Roggia corner. 'I'm OK, I'm fine,' he said, but he looked drawn and ashen faced. The accident, probably caused by the diffuser being damaged on a kerb, was a really bad one.

'I saw the Ferrari in the barrier and realised that Michael could have been hurt very badly,' reported Giancarlo Fisichella, who was not far behind the Ferrari in his Benetton.

'I was lucky not to hurt myself,' said Michael a few days later.

Ill fortune stayed with him at the start of the next race, the German Grand Prix at Hockenheim. This time, he was hit very hard by Luciano Burti in the Prost. The Ferrari got off the line well but after a few metres, suddenly slowed, let down by its gearbox. Burti had started from sixteenth place and was unable to avoid the collision. The impact was worse for him than for Schumacher but the result was the same, with both drivers out of the race. However, after one lap behind the safety car, the race was stopped because there was too much debris on the track, and Schumacher was able to make the restart in the spare car. Second time around, he did not fare much better, retiring on lap twenty-three with a fuel-pump problem. It was his second and final retirement in a near perfect season.

'I am lucky again. It could have been much worse when Burti rammed me from behind,' commented Michael.

He was also lucky in that Coulthard's engine problems meant he never made it to the flag and the gap stayed at thirty-seven points with five races to go. If Schumacher managed to score three points more than Coulthard in Hungary, at the height of summer, he would become world champion.

'What can I do against Martians? Schumacher is an extraterrestrial and the Ferrari is a car from another planet,' suggested David Coulthard after qualifying for the Hungarian Grand Prix where, just for a change, Schumacher had taken pole position. The 2001 Ferrari had little real opposition — it would have even less in 2002 but no one knew that at the time. The crowning glory, a second consecutive world title, was not far away now and Sunday would be a day for record breaking.

'My Ferrari is so perfect it even takes me by surprise,' Schumacher said. He may have let himself go a little in his comments but he was careful not to talk about winning just yet. 'We can expect a long and tiring race,' he added.

Of the seventy-seven laps that stood between him and the world title, the most dangerous was the one that did not count. Driving to the grid on Sunday afternoon, he lost control of the rear end of the car and, in order not to damage the F2001 on the kerbs, he ran wide through the gravel trap, bumping along to rejoin the track. When he arrived in position on the grid, the mechanics changed the barge boards and checked that everything else was all right.

'I was nervous,' Schumacher said by way of explanation. 'Usually, I have a sleep for half an hour before a race, but I didn't manage more than twenty minutes this time before waking up.' It might well have crossed David Coulthard's mind that even extraterrestrials have souls.

Once the race was under way, any nerves and fears vanished in an instant, helped by the fact that Rubens Barrichello was running behind Schumi, having started from the second row behind Coulthard. When the Scotsman managed to get past the Brazilian after the first pit stop, it was too late for him to set about chasing Schumacher. In the end, after the second and final pit stop, Barrichello moved back up to second place, which proved decisive in closing down the constructors' championship — another perfect race, another perfect result. The only factor Michael Schumacher could do nothing about was the tears. They started to flow as soon as he crossed the line, shouting emotionally over the radio — 'Thank you, thank you everyone. You are fantastic, amazing. I love you, I love all of you.'

Three hundred and fifteen days after entering the record books with his first Ferrari title, Michael Schumacher took another step towards legendary status — four world titles, fifty-one wins and two consecutive world championships with Ferrari, this last achievement equalling Alberto Ascari's. On such a Sunday, even for a man with an allergy to statistics, the numbers made happy reading.

He leapt from his car, hugged Alesi, Ralf and Barrichello and was congratulated by Hakkinen. He stood on his Ferrari and then jumped for joy on the top step of the podium as though he had springs on his feet. He raised his arms and blew kisses hither and thither. He looked for his mechanics, his engineers, while below him the Hungaroring tarmac was transformed into a sea of red. The fans streamed down from the hills and the flags blended in with the team's clothing, Italian flags mixed in with the German ones. When the sound of the Italian national anthem blasted out of the speakers, Schumi was overcome with emotion. Somehow he had held it back while the German anthem was playing, but now he could not contain himself. He was the happiest man in the world and he wanted everyone to know it. He had to tell those sitting in front of him in the press conference and he had to tell the TV viewers.

'I can do it with a steering wheel and I'm not bad as a driver, but I'm not so good when it comes to words. Please forgive me. Try to understand what I want to say and what I'm feeling as best you can. It was a fantastic, perfect weekend. Before coming here I didn't know that this would be the weekend for the championship. I don't know why, but I didn't feel it was the right one inside me. I was quickest on Friday, then on Saturday I took pole with an amazing time, but it was only after the warm-up, when I felt in perfect harmony with the car, that I realised this could be our day.'

He did not want to talk about his three other titles, and when asked about Fangio's record of five titles, which was now within his grasp, he replied, 'It's not possible to make a comparison. He won in an age when the cars were much more dangerous. He was very quick in cars I would be scared to drive.'

He wanted to talk about this particular triumph. 'It represents the efforts of the entire team. It has a warmth and humanity that I have never encountered anywhere else. After my wife and family, they are the most important people in my life. I love them all. I tried to tell them on the radio after the race when I was shouting with happiness.'

Naturally, his thanks also extended to Rubens Barrichello.

'It's not by chance that since he arrived, Ferrari has won everything. Thanks to him, I can rest more and spend more time with my family while testing is going on because I really know that Rubens does a good job on the track.'

In order to understand why one Ferrari victory now followed another, why a winning streak turned into an era, read this declaration from the newly crowned champion.

'I said it after winning the 2000 championship. My aim is to win as many races as possible. I still have three years on my contract with Ferrari and I would like to experience other days like this. I know that come the first mistake, people will not remember this victory, but will ask me why I made the mistake. In sport, only the present matters. And deep inside, I feel the fire that makes me want to continue racing and winning for a long time to come.'

Schumacher's fire is the same one that lights up Montezemolo, Todt, Martinelli, Brawn and Byrne, and motivates the man who cleans the wheels, the cook who prepares the pasta, and the men who drive the seven transporters that bring thirty tonnes of equipment to every grand prix.

'Our secret is that we like one another,' said Todt by way of attempting an explanation. 'We are united as a team of professionals at the highest level where everyone gives their all for the good of everyone else.'

'Enzo Ferrari would be proud of us and of this team,' Montezemolo added. He had come to Budapest to join the party in a downtown hotel. 'This win took some building,' continued the President. 'We are a big group and a big family, a company with amazing human qualities that knows how to combine its culture, tradition and history with modernising for the future. We are aware that we are living in a modern era. Following the death of Enzo Ferrari, there were years of putting our house in order and dealing with troubles. It was not easy for a company so closely linked to such a great man to make a painless transition from one phase to another. I believe that over the past three years, Ferrari have shown clear signs of a tremendous turnaround, achieved without losing touch with our historic and cultural past. This has allowed us to stand firm through difficult moments at the start of the nineties when there were calls for change and revolution. By digging in, the results came. The results were planned and worked for and did not drop out of the sky.'

'Planned and worked for' is the key phrase. On that triumphant night, on the sidelines of the party, Ross Brawn and others were already thinking of the future.

'We have entered the Ferrari era, but we must not look on the results of the past and the present as a guarantee for the future,' said Brawn. 'We must still put the same effort into our work. That is the only way we can prepare a sequel to this triumph for the Cavallino. Already we are concentrating on the design of next year's car. We know we have two great drivers and an equally strong team from a technical and human point of view. It's a good basis to continue in the same vein.'

Confirmation that Ferrari was not resting on its laurels came very soon. Just a fortnight after the Budapest party, in the Belgian Grand Prix, Michael Schumacher picked up win number fifty-two. No one had won more in over fifty years of Formula 1 racing. Alain Prost's record was now beaten.

'Any win at Spa is special,' reckoned Michael. 'Here and at Monaco, driver input counts for a lot and I like that. Just as I will really enjoy sitting in an armchair after I have stopped racing, lighting a cigar, having a beer and thinking that no one has won more races than me and that these fifty-two wins are a record.'

The win came his way relatively easily because those who had been quicker than him in qualifying were out of the running before the start. Montoya never made the first start, while Ralf was left up on jacks for the second.

'It wasn't nice when I turned round and saw that Ralf was up on the jacks. I would have enjoyed fighting with him and us being together on the podium,' commented Michael, seemingly hard to please. 'Continuing to win after having taken the championship is very nice. It shows we never give up and that this really is our year. Now comes Monza and going there as champions will be great for our fans. I can't wait to celebrate with them. But this time, Monza will give me mixed emotions. A friend of mine, Pepi, lived in Monza. He passed away recently. I will feel a great void.'

Pepi Cereda, a young journalist who worked with the Mediaset network, died just before the Belgian Grand Prix after a brief and terrible illness. Pepi was mad about Formula 1, and Formula 1 people, including Schumacher, had a small place for him in their hearts. This was the other side of Schumacher, the less well known one that he prefers to keep hidden. Schumacher the sensitive and generous human being does not shirk from suffering, regularly meeting people less fortunate than himself. He knows a champion can help others in a thousand ways, with a telephone call, a visit or a donation. In his role as an ambassador for UNESCO, he has never held back.

The world will never forget what happened a few days before the Italian Grand Prix — the vile terrorist attack on the Twin Towers in New York. Ferrari decided to remove all sponsor logos from the cars' bodywork and, as a sign of mourning, the nose sections were painted black. There were some who did not want to race at all, but that was not an option. The Americans themselves continued racing, staging a CART race in Europe at the Lausitzring that same weekend. At Monza on Saturday, the news and photos arrived from the German circuit, showing the terrible accident sustained by Alex Zanardi.

The next day, the feeling that the race should not take place increased. Schumacher was the main instigator of this idea and asked that, at the very least, drivers sign an agreement not to race one another through the first few corners, so as to reduce the risk of an accident at the first chicane. It was an emotional reaction at the end of a troubled week. However, it proved impossible to reach agreement on a course of action.

'It's sad. There are some drivers who cannot decide on their own, but who are made to obey team orders and go back on what we had already agreed. It was only a question of safety, to agree not to attack one another in the first two corners. It seems an intelligent choice,' commented Schumacher, who had not forgotten that one year earlier, a marshal had been killed here.

In the race itself, Michael made no effort to finish in a podium position, as if he did not want to celebrate with champagne or face the press in the mandatory press conference. Montoya won the race ahead of Barrichello, who was slowed by a problem with the refuelling rig. It was the Colombian's first Formula 1 win, but it was a sad occasion. There are those who say that if the fight for the world championship had still been on, Schumacher would have reacted differently. But for those who have come to know him and appreciate him for what he does away from the racetrack, this is not a viable suggestion.

After Monza came Indianapolis and a trip to the United States, a nation in a state of shock. Formula 1 decided to keep going because life must go on and the threat of terrorism must not be allowed to have a paralysing effect. The people of Indianapolis understood this and reacted in style. On race day, the grandstands were packed with 200,000 spectators. They had come to watch the grand prix, but also to show the world that America was not giving in.

The contest delivered Mika Hakkinen's final victory in the penultimate race of his career. He won from Schumacher, who had picked up another pole position but was caught napping by Montoya at the end of the main straight. Hakkinen also duelled enthusiastically with Barrichello until the Brazilian's engine failed.

'Hakkinen won it fair and square and I'm happy for him,' commented Schumi. 'But I feel sorry for Rubens who was let down by his engine just when it looked as though he could do it. It would have been much better if it had happened to me. It's a shame because we had worked out a different strategy, which meant he was running lighter than me and could have got ahead.' In essence, Ferrari had decided to reward Barrichello for all his hard work and gift him the win.

'Unlucky? It's not a word I like, but I felt a blow to the heart when my engine started to make strange noises,' commented Rubinho.

That left just one more chance, in the Japanese Grand Prix. A win would also propel him to second place in the championship, ahead of Coulthard, but it all ended under the sign of Schumacher. He took pole position, his eleventh, and the win, his ninth, meant he rounded off the year with 123 points. It seemed impossible to do better than this but Ferrari was blazing a legendary trail and the journey was far from over.

RACE DAY

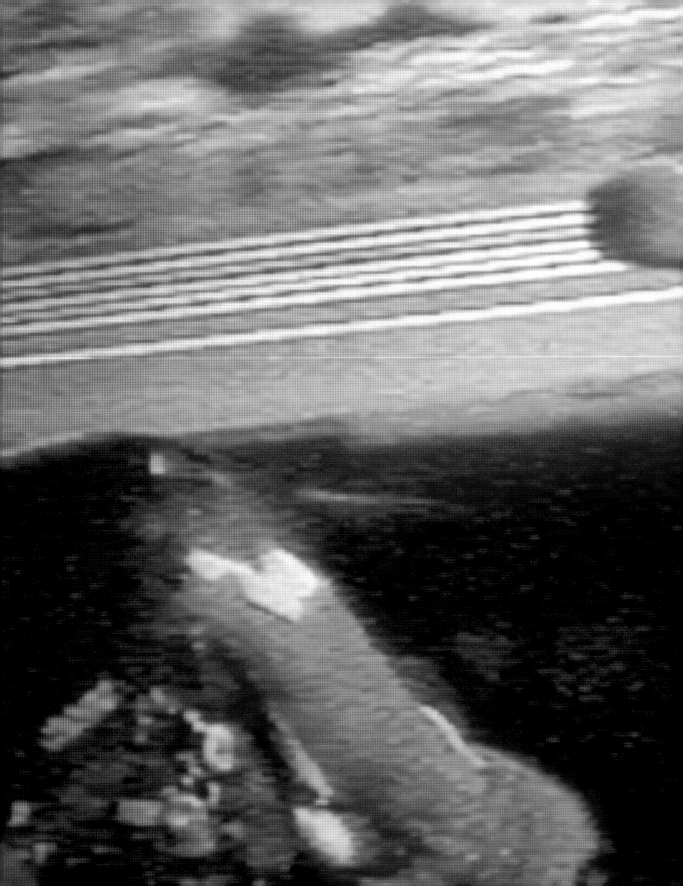

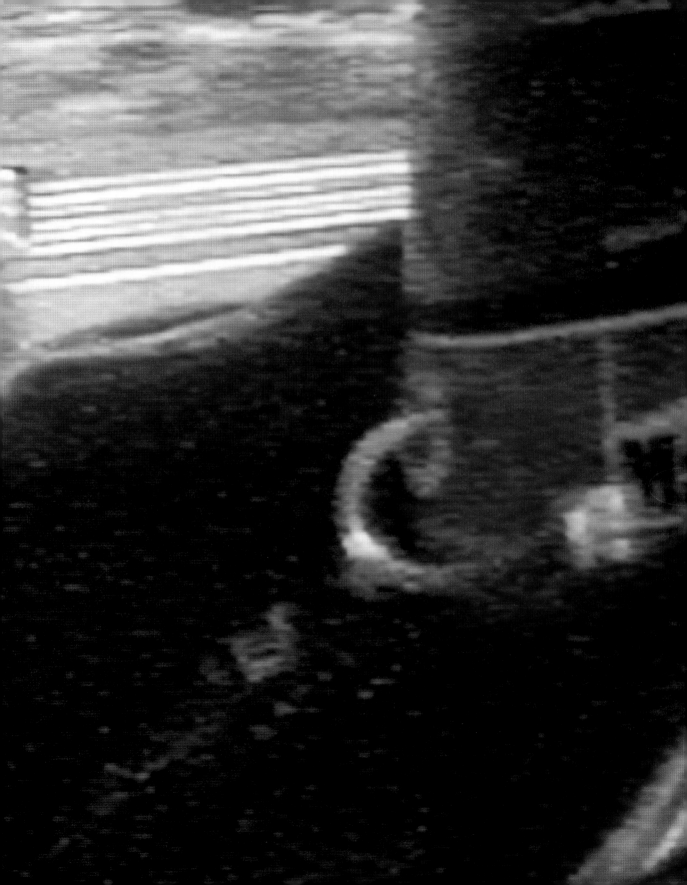

7

2002 – THE DICTATORSHIP

Schumacher equals Fangio

Sport, just like life, can throw up some magic moments when everything is going well and every move is the right one. That's how it was for Ferrari from the turn of the century, Schumacher and his crew achieving legendary status. If 2001 was an extraordinary year, 2002 came close to perfection. The drivers' championship was in the bag in July, after just eleven grands prix, with the constructors' title following in August in Hungary – fifteen wins from seventeen races, eleven of them for Schumacher, and a total of 221 points, the exact number scored by all the opposing teams put together. Schumacher finished on the podium in every single race, which meant that at least one Ferrari had finished in the top three for fifty-three grands prix, dating back to the 1999 Malaysian race.

After the great feast of 2001, there was absolutely no let up. Michael Schumacher spent the winter working on his fitness and checking on progress at the factory.

'Every two days he rings up for news on the new car, the new tyres and work in general,' revealed Todt and Brawn.

It gave everyone a boost, especially the mechanics, test driver Luca Badoer and his newly appointed co-worker Luciano Burti. Remarks made by Brawn, Byrne and Martinelli describing the new car as the 'best Ferrari ever' turned out to be prophetic. It proved to be almost unbeatable, and even went on to help Ferrari score precious points at the start of the 2003 season.

'I'll settle for winning both the championships again,' joked Montezemolo on the day the new car was shown to the world, 6 February. The presentation was held inside the futuristic Nuova Meccanica department, where the Ferrari and Maserati road-car engines are built in an environment that has a surprising mix of high technology and areas of greenery. Paolo Fresco and Paolo Cantarella represented Fiat at the launch. 'We have chosen to take risks, to present an innovative car rather than a simple evolution of last year's championship-winning model,' added the president.

The engineers explained further. 'It's all new,' they said. 'The aerodynamics feature smaller side pods, the gearbox is titanium, while the chassis is different in terms of both design and construction. The engine has a lower centre of gravity.' They were confident in their achievement and in the data acquired in the wind tunnel. The car was so futuristic compared with the opposition that it was enough to make the team dream of further success. The only thing missing at this stage was a word or two from the car itself as the engine had yet to be tested on the racetrack. Schumacher rectified the situation when at 9.52 a.m. on 10 February, he gave the signal for the engine to be fired up.

'At the end of that day, I was already convinced that the F2002 was the best Ferrari I had ever driven,' he recalls. It was indeed a fantastic car, immediately setting a new lap record of 58.620 seconds at Fiorano. The car would go on to leave an indelible mark on the history of Ferrari and Formula 1 but its running-in period did not go smoothly and its race debut was put back to the Brazilian Grand Prix, the third round of the season. However, while the F2002 was being put through its paces, work had continued on the previous year's car. Even on the day of the presentation, while Schumacher and Barrichello were pulling the dustsheet off the new creation, Badoer and Burti were pounding round Mugello in the F2001.

The old Ferrari was still good enough to make a clean sweep in the opening round in Australia against opposition running their new cars. Barrichello took pole position, beating Schumacher by five-thousandths of a second (30.8 centimetres), and the German went on to win the race the next day, leaving the fastest race lap to Kimi Raikkonen, who was making his debut with McLaren. Of course, the car had been revamped. It was lighter by five kilos, with updated electronics and a bigger fuel tank. The aerodynamics had been refined, while the engine was already a step on the way to the 051, which would power the F2002. Ferrari were more than capable of working on two fronts, running in the new car while getting the last drop of performance out of the old one.

Barrichello was finding it easier to cope with being team-mate to the best driver in the world. The Rubens who turned up in Melbourne was a more rounded character than the Rubens of the previous year.

'The birth of my son Eduardo has changed me,' he said. 'The happiness it has given me has removed a lot of tension from my life. I now feel happier about everything I do.'

However, as if dealing with one Schumacher on a daily basis was not enough, he came across another in the shape of Ralf at the start of the race. If Rubens and Ralf were trying to win at the very first corner, they were punished for their impatience, both being knocked out of the race when Ralf's Williams flew over Barrichello's Ferrari as they collided. Michael went wide to avoid the carnage, running on to the grass and dropping down the order to fourth place. He waited for the right moment to stage an inexorable fight back, profiting from Trulli's spin and passing Montoya to take the lead on lap seventeen and staying there to the flag. He drove an intelligent race. 'A perfect start,' commented the world champion. What else could he say?

With the old car still winning, there was no need to rush the new one into the fray. The idea of running one old and one new car in Malaysia was on the agenda for a few days but, having studied all the pros and cons, it was decided to stick with the revitalised F2001. In the end, victory in Sepang went to the younger Schumacher in his Williams-BMW. Michael started from pole and went on to finish third after a collision with Montoya at the first corner, followed by a long climb back up through the field. The Colombian was penalised by the stewards but, after the race, Michael absolved him of guilt.

'Juan Pablo is the sort who never gives up. He closed the door on me and I could not brake. The penalty he was given strikes me as a bit excessive,' was Michael's comment. Nevertheless, the fourteen points picked up in two races with the old Ferrari meant that Schumacher was already charging off in the championship lead. Barrichello, let down by his engine, had yet to score.

The result of the Malaysian Grand Prix, with Montoya's Williams recording the fastest lap and Schumacher finishing a minute down, convinced Ferrari to accelerate the programme to bring the F2002 to the races. Schumacher was particularly keen to use it immediately, even if there were still some doubts over the reliability of its titanium gearbox.

'It took a bit of doing to convince Ross,' he said, 'but at the end of the weekend, he agreed with me.'

The team took one F2002 to Brazil for Schumacher to drive and he won the race, although not from pole position, thus continuing the tradition of the previous few years. Started by Irvine in 1999 and followed by Schumacher in 2000 and 2001, all three times in Australia, the new car had won first time out. It would happen again in 2003, when Schumacher won in Barcelona, making five consecutive winning debuts. In the previous fifty years it had happened just four times — in 1952 in Switzerland with Taruffi, in 1956 in Argentina with Fangio and Musso, in 1979 in South Africa with Villeneuve and in 1989 in Brazil with Mansell.

Schumacher and the F2002 caught everyone napping immediately after the start, when the Ferrari shot ahead of Montoya's Williams. The overtaking move happened at the Senna 'S' corner and the Colombian was so surprised that his reaction was definitely and excessively wrong. He hit the Ferrari, which emerged unscathed, but the Williams had to pit to have its bent front wing changed. Schumacher was going at such a pace that it fooled his brother Ralf into thinking that Michael was planning to make an extra pit stop and was driving so quickly because he had less fuel on board. How wrong can you be? The new Ferrari turned out to be a little marvel.

At one point, Michael was overtaken by Barrichello in the old car, but Rubens was stopping once more than the others. Having started from eighth, it was the only possible strategy for him. The Brazilian had a great time during some sixteen laps, passing Raikkonen, Coulthard, Button, Ralf and Michael Schumacher, but hydraulic problems cut in and the F2001 was brought to a halt for the last time and parked at the side of the track, having led the field for the last two laps of its competition career.

From then on, Schumacher drove an extraordinary race with Ralf stuck behind him for the last twenty-six laps, unable to find the slightest gap to slip by his big brother. Michael was so quick that he even caught out football legend Pele, who was charged with waving the chequered flag. The photo of Pele not showing the flag as Schumacher whizzed right under his nose became the symbol of this Brazilian Grand Prix and of a world championship that seemed to be completely one-sided. The Ferraris would continue to leave the opposition scrabbling in their wake. Formula 1 had become Formula Ferrari.

Schumacher and his F2002 won four grands prix in a row — Brazil, San Marino, Spain and Austria — romping away with the championship. Imola was the first race where both drivers had use of the F2002 and they promptly scored the first one-two finish of the season, with Schumacher ahead of Barrichello, as Ferrari beat Ferrari.

'Maximum joy for our fans,' commented Montezemolo.

'I have been with Ferrari since 1996 and the team has constantly improved. No one can match our motivation. This year's car is fantastic and has not yet realised its full potential. Both in Brazil and here, I expected to have to fight hard for the win, but it came almost easily. With this car we will amaze you, amaze everyone,' maintained Schumacher.

Alongside him and Barrichello on the podium stepped one of the fathers of the new car, Rory Byrne.

'Rory is exceptional both in human terms and professionally,' said Schumacher. 'I am proud to continue working with someone like him.'

Finally, Barrichello was also happy. It was the first time that season he had finished a race and he did it in style with second place. 'It's my first podium as a dad and so I have to dedicate it to little Eduardo,' he said.

In Spain, at the track where he scored his first victory in a Ferrari back in 1996, Schumacher continued his winning streak — pole position, fastest race lap and third consecutive win with the new car. The reigning champion's declaration of love was inevitable.

'You have given me a magic Ferrari, a dream car. Thanks, thanks to all the team for the work you have done. I am very happy…'

Not so happy was Rubens Barrichello, who was stranded on the starting grid with an electrical problem.

'I pressed every single button on the steering wheel but the car just didn't want to know,' he said.

It seemed that Michael had problems only when there was still time to do something about them, whereas with Rubens that never seemed to be the case. The Spanish Grand Prix provided a classic example of this. Schumacher had a problem with his car during the morning warm-up, raced with the spare car and won. Barrichello's troubles surfaced when he was already on the grid.

In Austria a fortnight later, Barrichello had the opportunity to try again. On a track of which his team-mate has never been particularly fond, Rubens started from pole position and stayed in the lead for almost the entire race. However, with only a few laps to go, a call came over the radio from Ross Brawn, instructing him to let Michael, who was better placed in the championship, pass. Brawn's instruction fell on deaf ears and so Todt had to repeat it. This time, Rubens obeyed and, just before the chequered flag, he moved over for his team-mate, the transparency of the action making it even more controversial.

Schumacher was clearly surprised by the reaction to his win, first of all on the podium and then in the press conference. During the prize-giving, in a sincere but vain attempt to deal with the booing, he left his team-mate on the top step of the podium as the German national anthem was being played. Then, in the media centre, taken aback by a mass of questions critical of him and Ferrari, Michael stated that he had thought of disobeying the order. 'I am not happy with this win,' he went on. 'It's possible we made the wrong decision.'

However, that same evening, Michael called Todt, who had just landed at Bologna airport, to apologise for his behaviour after the race. Clearly, both drivers were aware of the team policy. So, even before the race began, they could have expected that, if they found themselves in this position in the final laps, they would have to swap places.

With hindsight, Ferrari would probably never take such a decision again although in the days following the race they defended their position, especially after the futile inquiry set up by the FIA and the inevitable protestations from rival teams. The Austrian Grand Prix was the sixth round of the championship and the difference between first and second place was four points. In winning, Schumacher extended his lead over Montoya to twenty-seven points. If he had settled for second, his lead would have been twenty-three. Knowing how the championship finally ended, one can criticise the decision, but bearing in mind the situation at the end of the nineties when championships were lost at the last race and results compromised by accidents, it is possible to understand the thinking behind the team's action. Without condoning it, it is hard to condemn it, but that decision continues to be a small black mark on an otherwise perfect season.

At the European Grand Prix one month later, the men from Maranello did not make the same mistake again. Jean Todt gave no orders to Barrichello as he headed for victory with Schumacher right behind. Rubens had taken pole on the way to the second win of his career.

'Thanks for making me win,' he joked over the radio, having crossed the finish line.

This time there were no team orders for at least three reasons. The situation in the championship table was now much clearer. Second place in Monaco and victory in Canada meant that Schumacher was on seventy points with Ralf and Montoya stuck on twenty-seven. Criticism after Austria had been so severe that there was no way the team would spark off another controversy, and a few days after the Nurburgring race, the FIA was due to meet in Paris to discuss the Austrian affair. The tribunal 'acquitted' Ferrari of wrong doing on the track, but imposed a mega fine of one million dollars, with half suspended, for not observing the correct protocol during the podium ceremony. No penalty was dished out for ordering Barrichello to let Schumacher win.

'I can't say I'm happy with the earthquake provoked by the company decision at the A1-Ring,' Todt confessed once the championship was won. 'The booing affected me a lot. At least the way we went about it was honest and transparent. I don't know if I would take such a decision again, even if I am a Ferrari man through and through and the good of the company always comes first. Maybe I'm wrong to think like this, but the interests of the Scuderia are always my number one priority.'

By the time the European Grand Prix came round, the championship was virtually wrapped up. Schumacher's lead was such that no orders were required. Even in Monaco, where the win eluded him, Schumacher managed to extend his championship lead by coming home second. The race was won by David Coulthard in his McLaren, but he was not a title challenger. In Canada, after Montoya took pole, Schumacher scored Ferrari's 150th victory, putting him into a conclusive lead. After that, it was simply a case of choosing at which race to celebrate winning the title.

Schumacher moved things forward by winning at Silverstone ahead of Barrichello in another classic red one-two finish. For Michael, win number sixty in his career owed much to an intuitive strategy from the pit wall. When the rain intensified on lap thirteen, Schumacher and Barrichello were switched to intermediate tyres, while Montoya, after a fourth consecutive pole, opted for wets. Schumacher flew to the flag. Barrichello had an electrical problem on the formation lap and was forced to start from the back of the grid, but managed to claw his way up to second, with Montoya dropping away to come home third, thirty seconds down.

Schumacher attributed much of the credit for this win on English soil, home to Ferrari's main rivals, to Ross Brawn, the man on the pit wall. Munching away on bananas, he took the right decisions and in recognition of his role, Todt sent the Englishman up to the podium to collect the Scuderia's trophy.

'Ross was really great,' eulogised Schumacher. 'He made the decision to change my tyres at just the right moment and to go on to intermediates. I was not really convinced at the time, but he insisted and he was right. I was still making up my mind when Ross called me in over the radio to go for the less risky solution. Then after the stop, he guided me over the radio and I was able to concentrate on overtaking Montoya.'

It was a real team effort, turning the situation around at the most difficult moment. As Ross Brawn explained, the rain caught everyone by surprise.

'Obviously, we got our weather forecast wrong,' he admitted. 'We had no indication of rain for the race and we therefore ran the cars with dry weather settings. So when the rain got stronger, we had no other choice than to fit the intermediate tyres.'

It was the expectation of a dry race that led Schumacher to question Brawn's decision, but Ross insisted and was right to do so.

'I have a really fantastic team,' commented Schumacher.

Silverstone was yet another demonstration of the importance of having a strong team behind the drivers. Michael Schumacher and Ross Brawn now have such a degree of understanding that a look, a word, a gesture is all that is required between them. They have worked together since Schumacher's second-ever Formula 1 race at Monza in 1991 and were apart only for the German's first year in Maranello in 1996. The understanding between the men in the Ferrari pits becomes even more apparent in the light of what happened in the neighbouring pits during the British Grand Prix, with radio communication interfering with the telemetry, tyres going missing and cars running out of fuel.

With 'a glass of red wine and a good cigar' is how Michael Schumacher recalls celebrating win number sixty. What he could not remember was the last time he failed to finish a race. It took him a while to think of it — 'almost a year ago in Hockenheim when my fuel pump failed'. Since then, he had won ten races, been on the podium fourteen times and had fifteen points finishes. Record followed record. Now the record of the legendary Juan Manuel Fangio loomed on the horizon. He could clinch the championship in France on 21 July in the eleventh round of the season and if he did so, he would equal Fangio. He would also better Nigel Mansell's record, achieved in 1992, of becoming champion on 16 August in Hungary, with five races remaining to the end of the season.

With the whiff of world titles in the air, Schumacher began the weekend that would guarantee him another mention in the record books with three spins in a row. 'Nervous? No, I was just pushing too hard,' he explained. But Michael did not excel in Saturday's qualifying, also incurring a penalty that robbed him of his best lap time for having missed the chicane. It fell to Juan Pablo Montoya, who was on pole for a fifth consecutive time, to try to delay Ferrari's celebrations.

'Starting from second is not too much of a drama and I'm still not thinking about the title,' bluffed Schumacher.

In truth, he knew only too well that if he increased his championship lead from fifty-four to sixty points, he would be world champion. Mathematically still in with a chance of top honours were Barrichello (fifty-four points behind), Montoya (fifty-five behind) and Ralf Schumacher (fifty-six behind). If Michael won with Barrichello or Montoya second, he would have to delay the festivities.

Barrichello was out of the running before the start, failing to get off the line at the start of the formation lap, but Montoya was up for a fight. He went off in the lead and stayed there until the first pit stop when Schumacher got past him but picked up a drive-through penalty because he crossed the white line when leaving the pit lane. He lost two places, dropping to third behind Montoya and Raikkonen. It seemed the champagne would have to be kept on ice.

However, the Colombian began to drop back, and with him no longer in the chase for the podium, the only obstacle standing between Schumacher and a fifth world title was Raikkonen, who moved into the lead on the fifty-fourth of seventy-two laps. Only a win would give Schumacher the championship. With four laps remaining, Raikkonen gifted him big time. He slid off the track at the Adelaide corner on oil spewed out when Allan McNish's Toyota engine blew up. The door was open and Schumacher had no option but to go through it, even though yellow flags were being waved. He would have had to come to a complete stop to avoid making a passing move, as the Finn was so far off the track. Anyone could see that no rules had been infringed. The chequered flag and history awaited Schumacher.

When the Italian and German anthems rang out, Schumi, already drenched in champagne, could not hold back the emotion.

'Michael cried all the way round the last lap. He was crying so much, he couldn't talk on the radio,' confessed Ross Brawn, who lived through the race with Michael, minute by minute, moment by moment.

'I had a premonition and was convinced that I would take the championship only in Hockenheim,' said Schumacher. 'The way the race was going, I didn't think this was my day. First there was Rubens' problem, then Montoya was in front of me for a long time and then I made a mistake after the first stop when I crossed the white line and got the penalty. That happened because I was concentrating on Montoya, who was chasing me, and I was watching my mirrors. From the pit wall, Brawn told me about it, so I tried to push hard to build up an advantage so that the penalty did not affect me too much.

'When I was back on track I was surprised to find I was second behind Kimi. There were ten laps to go and I decided to give it my all again to put him under pressure. Then Kimi skidded on the oil. There was nothing he could do. I had been warned about the oil from McNish's Toyota and so I was able to react a bit. He was unaware of the danger and went off the track.

'The last few laps were the worst of my career and I could feel the weight of an enormous responsibility. I was scared of making a mistake and ruining everything.'

That account of events provides an insight into the work of the men on the Ferrari pit wall. They need four eyes to get the job done, watching the timing screens, the television, the telemetry data and the track. Everything has to be under control to give the drivers as clear a picture as possible. Michael and Rubens concentrate on the driving while the engineers worry about everything else. Todt, Brawn, Domenicali and the race engineers each have their monitors, computers and radio headsets. They are virtual drivers alongside Schumi and Barrichello, like navigators with rally drivers. That was how Michael knew that he had to be careful at the Adelaide corner because of the oil, and why he was in a position to capitalise on Raikkonen's mistake.

Michael wanted to share the moment with those who had helped him.

'Fangio was a great man and I cannot compare myself with him. He didn't have this incredible team behind him. I'm not a legend — this team is a legend. How do I feel? At a time like this it's difficult for me to find the right words. I have never managed it and this is overwhelming. It's incredible to race with this team and to win the title for them. I love them all, I love Ferrari, from the mechanics to the president, but I will not name anyone because I would have to remember the names of all the six hundred people who work in the Gestione Sportiva, with whom I enjoy a friendship that is impossible to describe. What we have achieved together over the past years is amazing. And now, I'm ready for more challenges, more titles and more wins.' His speech captured the mood within Ferrari. 'Every win is special, each one is important and all of them are different, but I cannot tell you which one is the most important for me,' he added.

Both declarations, made in the heat of the moment, highlighted his love for Ferrari and his incredible will to continue winning, two key elements in creating the team's spirit. The feelings were mutual. The teamwork is based on an unquenchable thirst for victory — another reason why Ferrari had not lost since 1999.

Apart from Ferrari, Schumi was also keen to thank his wife publicly.

'Behind the success of any man, whatever he does for a living, the support of the woman by his side is fundamental. I don't need to tell you how important Corinna is to me. She has played a big part in this win, as she did in the others, but this time, she was even more important. She ensured I was very calm as the day came near. Corinna keeps me grounded and this is marvellous. She is not just my wife, she is also my best friend.'

Corinna stays close without being invasive; she is affectionate without being suffocating and she is happy to share his joy.

'This is fantastic,' she said. 'But it has not sunk in yet — a five times world champion. It's crazy. If he's having fun, then so am I.'

A week after the great event, he was back on track again for the German Grand Prix.

'As a driver, I have won the world championship, so now it's time to have fun. That means I will try to win, especially here in front of my fans, where my record is not so good. I have won just once,' declared the newly crowned champion.

With one target reached, there were still two more to achieve — winning the constructors' championship and ensuring that Barrichello came second in the drivers' classification. In order to help Rubens, it was decided to allocate him the spare car for the final races of the season. That recognition of all his hard work was also a sign of how the team planned to stay united.

'I welcome the decision about the spare car,' commented Rubens, 'but it's obvious that Ferrari will never tell Michael to slow down. First of all, I must try to drive quickly because if I'm behind, there will be nothing else to do about it. It's great working with Ferrari because they respect you and give you a great car to drive.'

'Now that the pressure of winning the world championship has gone, my motivation is even stronger,' declared Schumi.

Barrichello knew what he was up against. Michael never gives up and in front of his home crowd, he took pole position and went on to win the race ahead of Montoya and Ralf. Rubens was fourth, unlucky once again. First of all, he had to switch to the spare car as there was a problem with the gearbox on his race machine. Then, at the pit stop, he lost precious seconds and a podium finish when the fuel filler flap refused to open. As usual, all the celebrations were for his team-mate, and his goal of second place in the championship was still five points away.

'I thank God for allowing me to experience this,' said Schumi after the race, much to everyone's surprise. 'You cannot imagine how much I wanted this win. In the last few years, the German Grand Prix has always escaped me and not gone my way, even though it means so much to me.' He was insatiable, like a kid who doesn't want to leave the funfair or his favourite toyshop. Michael continued to have a ball, and so too did everyone at Ferrari.

'We will do all we can to help Barrichello come second in the drivers' championship,' stated Jean Todt, another perfectionist in the camp, and come Hungary, Rubens was on winning form. He came home first ahead of Schumacher, and that was enough to give the team the constructors' title.

'This is the greatest and most exciting victory in Ferrari's racing history,' enthused Montezemolo. 'Words cannot do justice to a season like this. I can only say on this occasion that I am proud of the people at Ferrari. Such success, the seventh title in four seasons, including drivers' and constructors', is very important for a company that earns its living making cars. And it is all down to our people.'

'I always said I would do all I could to help Rubens to pick up the ten points,' added Schumacher. 'There was no real reason to attack him, especially as on this track there is a big difference between being quicker and being able to overtake. And don't forget that Rubens can drive very quickly, so I could not really have overtaken him because he was always able to keep up a fast pace and did not give me the slightest opportunity. He drove a great race and deserves the win. It was also a fantastic day for me as we took the constructors' title with great style and a nice one-two finish. So, on the podium, I was very happy for Rubens, yes really very happy and for the title, too.'

As for the winner, he claimed to be 'over the moon because I have already been on the moon when I took my other wins'.

Everyone was happy. It was like a fairytale. Ferrari was living a fairytale existence where everything worked to perfection, all elements slotting into place.

'Well, it's more a case of meticulous preparation,' protested Ross Brawn. 'In Formula 1, a lack of problems is not down to miracles or luck. There's no secret. Reliability is the key to winning. Our first objective at the Hungaroring was to win the constructors' title. We got it and, with the one-two finish, Rubens has moved into second place in the drivers' championship. Now we are working on maintaining that position to the end of the season. It would be another wonderful result for Ferrari. We can do it and Rubens' determination is the best weapon we have in that respect.

'At Maranello, we prepare our great performances. We like to fight and win because we don't want to give best to our rivals. Formula 1 is a continuous challenge and it's easy to slip off the top. So we do all we can to stay at the same level of competitiveness. We will prepare for the remaining four races with the same attention to detail as always with the aim of continuing to win.'

That's easy to say but Ferrari were true to their word and completed the season in style. The perfect year ended in triumph with four more wins, four more one-two finishes to be precise — Schumi ahead of Barrichello in Belgium, Barrichello ahead of Schumi in Italy and Indianapolis and Schumi ahead of Rubinho in Japan. Rubens duly finished second in the championship. There was a certain inevitability to it, given the superiority of the F2002.

'This Ferrari really is from another planet, a sort of UFO rather than just a car,' exclaimed Schumacher. 'There were plenty of reasons to be optimistic at the start of the season, but we could never have imagined such a year. It's a special pleasure to drive a car like this. I'm a hundred per cent happy with it. I can't find the slightest fault with it. Maybe the only fault is that it will now be difficult to design a car that can do better than this.'

Quick, reliable and fantastic were the words Schumacher used when he faced the microphones after crossing the line in Belgium to take his tenth win of the season, beating Nigel Mansell's record. The Englishman had won nine grands prix in 1992 and Schumacher had already equalled this feat on two occasions. This was indeed the season of all the records. Nothing escaped Ferrari.

'Our strength is that we are never satisfied,' explained Martinelli, the man in charge of the engines. 'Look at what has happened this season. After winning the title in Magny-Cours, Schumacher drove with even more spirit, even more speed in Germany. In Hungary, where Barrichello won, Michael set a lap record with a perfect lap. At Ferrari, from the president down, no one ever gives up. After we have won a grand prix, we study the results to see if we could have done better.'

That philosophy is ingrained in every member of the Prancing Horse team. Every grand prix constitutes a new challenge. Every race is tackled as though the team has never won anything, which explains the fifty-three consecutive podium finishes between 1999 and 2002.

'Every time we finish in the top three it gives us enormous satisfaction,' added Martinelli. 'A podium finish represents a marvellous tribute to the work of all our engineers because keeping a Formula 1 car competitive over a long period of time demands a huge amount of work and effort.'

The winning streak continued at Monza, the home race, where there was certainly no shortage of motivation. The grandstands were a mass of red with the crowd cheering every time a Ferrari went past. Imagine the frenzy when Barrichello went into the lead with Schumacher lining up behind him. It was the apotheosis. The main straight at the national circuit was transformed as the fans invaded the track beneath the new podium, the ideal place to get the party started.

'It was a unique experience. Perched above that sea of red I felt like a rock star at a concert,' said Rubens Barrichello after taking his third win of the season. 'Towards the end, I was screaming over the radio. I was singing a Brazilian song at the top of my voice. The mechanics are used to it. They know I sing when I'm happy. I even do it during test sessions when things are going particularly well. Of course I was going to sing on a day like this.'

Those test sessions were another factor in Ferrari's run of wins. With almost all the opposition switching to Michelin, Ferrari were the only top team running on Bridgestone tyres and the Maranello crew pretty much doubled their testing efforts. Luciano Burti was taken on to help Badoer, who could no longer carry out all the work alone, and in 2003 along came Felipe Massa. The test sessions, whether the race drivers or the test drivers are at the wheel, are like mini grands prix, prepared for with meticulous attention to detail and precision. A set programme has to be followed in order to acquire the required data. After the Italian Grand Prix, even though the drivers' and constructors' titles were in the bag, Schumacher was on parade at Mugello for testing duties. 'We never stop,' he explained.

'In life, one must always try to improve,' added Jean Todt.

After Monza came Indianapolis. From the temple of European motor racing to the American version, in the country that represents Ferrari's biggest market for road-car sales. Schumacher and Barrichello dominated the race from the first to the last lap. They approached the finish line almost side by side, separated by just eleven-thousandths of a second or seven tiny centimetres. The result required a photo finish to determine the winner and, surprisingly, it turned out to be Rubens Barrichello.

'It was all down to me,' confessed Schumacher. 'I wanted to cross the line at the same time as Rubens, just like in a kart race. Rubens realised what I was doing and drew alongside, but he got ahead by the tiniest of margins.'

'I was not given any orders,' confirmed Rubinho. 'It all happened at the last corner when I was in his slipstream and he slowed down. I came up alongside and tried to look at him to see what he was planning. He didn't look at me, but braked again and so I thought he wanted me to go past to pay me back for what I had done for him in Austria.'

And so it ended with the two Ferraris practically joined together, parading past the chequered flag. For fans of the Cavallino, that historic image brought back memories of a famous photo taken in 1967 at Daytona when sporting director Franco Lini organised a parade finish with three Ferraris after twenty-four hours of racing.

Victory at Indy meant Barrichello could not be beaten for second place in the championship. He had never before finished that far up the order. 'It is very important for me and also for Ferrari, who can truly claim to have been totally dominant,' emphasised the Brazilian.

With every box ticked, there was still no chance that Ferrari would consider anything other than finishing the record-breaking season with one last win. Their rivals were under no illusions and at Suzuka on 13 October Michael Schumacher stamped his authority on the perfect season. Naturally, Rubens Barrichello was right behind. This was Schumacher's eleventh victory and the fifteenth for the team. It was also the fifteenth one-two finish for this partnership and Schumacher-Barrichello overtook the Senna-Prost combination in the record books.

'It is very difficult to find the words to describe a season like this,' commented the champion. 'To sum up, I could say that at first we were lucky, then after Austria, we overcame a difficult moment, even though we had not harmed anyone. And finally, having won the title so early, I could enjoy myself like a mad thing driving in the last races. Racing without the pressure of having to get the results was really great, a unique experience for me so far, and one that will probably never happen again.'

FERRARI FAN DAY, MUGELLO, 19 OCTOBER 2003

8

2003 — SCHUMACHER AND FERRARI REWRITE HISTORY

The never-ending Ferrari era

A fifth consecutive constructors' world championship and a sixth world title, the fourth consecutive one, for Michael Schumacher, who thus overtook Fangio's record of five world championships — these are the bare facts. Behind them lies the story of how, in 2003, Ferrari rewrote history, reaching a level that is unlikely to be matched in the future.

The triumph is recorded in countless photos — Schumacher, Barrichello and Todt hugging one another in brotherly embrace, Montezemolo's fatherly gesture of patting a toddler dressed in red at Maranello, and a group photo with the team united around the champions — all of which offer perfect illustrations of this team's spirit.

The television cameras captured another example when, on the sixth lap of the Japanese Grand Prix, having hit Takuma Sato, Michael Schumacher came back to the pits with his front wing missing. The accident compromised his chances of victory in the grand prix and also brought his title hopes into question but, in the Ferrari pits, no one panicked. Massimo Trebbi, the mechanic charged with placing the jack under the front end to lift the car, immediately realised this would not work because of the damage caused in the impact with the BAR. So what did he do? He threw the jack to one side and, with a great show of strength, lifted the front of the car by hand so that the nose section could be replaced, as four other mechanics rushed to help him. There was the essence of a winning team — knowing how to get out of trouble whatever the circumstances.

'Over the years, we have improved a lot in the way we work in the pits. We train regularly and even have a reserve team, like substitutes in a football match, in case someone has an accident or cannot come to a race. And we also practise by simulating the most critical and dangerous situations,' explained Ross Brawn. Apart from the episode at Suzuka, he cited the example of Austria when, with lightning-fast reactions, the mechanics intervened with fire extinguishers to deal with the flames that licked around the fuel nozzle on Schumacher's car. As Rory Byrne maintains, the team is united, having become tightly knit during the hard times when the titles were lost at the last hurdle.

'Making mistakes was part of the learning process on the way to proving almost perfect in the pit stops,' Stefano Domenicali elucidates further. 'Remember the mess at the Nurburgring in '99 when time was lost looking for a missing tyre for Eddie Irvine. We were able to react in a constructive way to that, without blaming the person responsible, only trying to work out why he had gone wrong. In this type of activity, improvisation is a nightmare! Everyone must have his role and carry it out to perfection. If you see that the person next to you is in trouble, you can't stop what you're doing to help him because that would only add to the delay and compound the errors. Everyone must carry out the job allocated to them to perfection and so we study on paper and in training how to react when a situation gets complicated.'

Ferrari unveiled the car that would mount the assault on a definitive entry in the Formula 1 record books on 7 February, with one notable absentee. Gianni Agnelli died in Turin on 24 January. Montezemolo and Todt had discussed what they could do to honour a man who would be sadly missed by Ferrari, and that led to thoughts of giving the car a special name. Several ideas were put forward, including F1GA, which was hastily thrown out as 'figa' in Italian is definitely not a word to bandy about in polite society! It was named the F2003–GA. Montezemolo was genuinely moved as he explained the reason behind the dedication, this gift to a friend who was no longer with the team but would always remain in the hearts of so many Italians.

In fact, the name tag was an additional burden because it meant that the car really did have to win — not easy as the opposition was getting very close and ready to overtake. Montezemolo was not about to leave anything to chance, not even the date of the presentation. It fell on a Friday and a curt note was sent to the press office — 'Check if we have ever launched a car on a Friday before and then check how the car went that year.' Research revealed no bad signs. The 1998 machine had been presented to the world on a Friday and was a well-born car.

'Our main objective when designing a new car is to make it quicker than the previous year's,' Rory Byrne reiterated. 'So far, we have always managed it. The F2003–GA is better than the F2002, which won so much. If the new car does not win as much, that's down to the strength of the opposition.'

Once again, in 2003 Ferrari opted for the same strategy employed the previous year, starting off the season using the old car, which was still very quick and certainly more reliable than the new one. The new rules, which banned virtually all work on the car between qualifying and the race, influenced the decision.

The F2003–GA started breaking records immediately. On its track debut on 11 February, it set a new lap record for Fiorano, covering seventy-eight trouble free laps and going round in under the old record time no less than seventeen times. 'Avvocato Agnelli would have been proud of this car,' commented Schumi, who nevertheless felt no need to hurry forward with its development programme. The car's race debut was scheduled for Imola and it was pointless to change the plans.

'A car can be quick immediately, but speed is not enough. There are other parameters that have to be met before using it in a race,' explained the technicians. However, a good car can be spotted right from the start and the F2003–GA was showing well with record times and few problems, at least that was the case until it was taken to Imola for its first test on a championship racetrack. Here, surprisingly, the F2002 was quicker. Development work on the championship-winning car had not stopped and Ferrari could therefore start the season with a car that was still competitive. It was best not to hurry with the new car, especially as, in Jerez, Luca Badoer suffered a bad crash at 280 km/h, caused by a technical problem.

'At least it wasn't as bad as in Barcelona two years ago, when I flipped over. It was a heavy impact, but I got away with just a few bruises,' the Scuderia's test driver said later.

Badoer has racked up the kilometres for Schumacher and Barrichello. Since 1998, he has done over 20,000 a year and his efforts regularly draw praise from Michael Schumacher.

'Driving for Ferrari means you can sit behind the wheel of the championship-winning car and that's a crazy feeling,' Luca went on. 'When I'm asked to define Ferrari, all I can say is that this is the perfect team and the perfect company. During testing, the atmosphere is always very professional. Win or lose, it doesn't change anything. When we take to the track for testing, the concentration is always at a maximum and the will to work and progress never changes. The Ferrari group's philosophy is always to work to the maximum and never back off. The best example is Schumacher himself.'

The work of the test driver, just like that of Schumacher and Barrichello, has its dangers. Badoer has risked his life at least three times with Ferrari, two of them within the space of a few weeks at the start of 2003. After the first incident in Jerez came another at Mugello at one of its most difficult corners, Le Arrabbiate.

'I saw the wall coming towards me and I thought this is it, but the next day I was desperately keen to get back on the track. It's always like that. For a minute after an accident you think about stopping, then the very next day, when you still ache all over, you already want to get back to work,' explained the man from Montebelluna.

Over the years he has gained the trust of Schumi, Barrichello and the team and is often charged with trying new parts that Schumacher and Barrichello will use for the first time in a race.

'Working alongside Schumacher, I have learnt so much from a technical point of view, and about his mentality and application to the job. The secret of his success? He's a little bit better than the rest in every area. In races it's crazy because no one can manage three hundred kilometres at qualifying pace the way Michael can.'

The new championship regulations came into force on 4 March, in time for the Australian Grand Prix in Melbourne. As reigning world champion, it fell to Schumacher to be first out of the pits for Friday's qualifying session.

'I got irritated with being the road sweeper and the track was very dirty,' he commented, which went some way towards explaining why he was seven-tenths of a second down on Barrichello. Thanks to his fastest time on Friday, Rubens won the right to go last on Saturday in the real grid-deciding session. It ended with an all-red front row. With Schumacher first, Barrichello second and Montoya almost a second off pole, it looked as though Ferrari were already in the driving seat. In the race, things turned out very differently.

Barrichello was penalised for jumping the start, but before he could pit to sit out his drive-through, he spun, hit the barrier and retired. Schumacher took off in the lead but not only did the win elude him, he finished fourth.

'The tyres, the safety car, Raikkonen's pace, having to pit to check the barge boards damaged on the kerbs — there were plenty of reasons why I didn't win,' explained the man in question.

Not since 26 September 1999, effectively in another century, had Ferrari failed to get at least one of its drivers on to the podium. After fifty-three grands prix, the magic run had come to an end. The result sounded the alarm bells and gave the impression that 2003 might not exactly be a stroll in the park.

The same thing happened again in Malaysia and Sao Paulo. Never before had Schumacher failed to make the podium for three races in a row and, fortunately for him, those races were not dominated by one driver. The spoils of victory were shared between Coulthard, Raikkonen and Fisichella.

In Brazil, the race was stopped after a rash of accidents in the rain — even Schumi went off the track — but there was a mistake in calculating the final lap. Race officials erroneously opted for lap fifty-five rather than fifty-six. The rules state that, when a race is stopped, the final result rests on positions two laps before the end. Raikkonen was leading on lap fifty-three, Fisichella on fifty-four, so Raikkonen was declared the winner. However, when the chequered flag was shown to the racers, Fisichella, still in the lead, had already started the next lap and, in the end, that was enough to give him the win. Ten days later, the FIA appeal tribunal in Paris watched footage of the race and awarded Fisichella the first grand prix win of his career. This suited Ferrari because it meant that Raikkonen, the initial leader of the championship, now had two points less to his name.

On the eve of the San Marino Grand Prix, Michael Schumacher had just eight points while his new rival already had twenty-four. Ferrari had to react and react quickly but, contrary to the original plan, at Imola they again had to make do with the old car. The running-in problems with the new F2003-GA still left a question mark hanging over its reliability and after a long series of tests at Fiorano and Mugello, the technical committee preferred to delay its race debut.

Schumacher was philosophical about the decision. The outside world was already talking about a crisis but he dismissed this idea in his own way, by laying down a declaration of faith in Ferrari and its crew and with another extraordinary performance on the track.

'We've lost some points that could have come our way, but I'm confident, relaxed and absolutely optimistic,' he said. 'This is the same Ferrari team that encountered difficulties from '96 to '98 and knew how to react by winning so many consecutive championships. The team knows how to do it this time as well. Objectively, we're not in difficulty, we're just lacking the results. I'm being positive and I have not forgotten that last year at Imola, the F2002 scored a fantastic one-two finish.'

However, the Imola weekend rapidly turned into one of deep sadness for the Schumacher family, especially Michael and Ralf, who never forget they are brothers as well as rivals. From Germany came desperate news about their mother. Elisabeth Schumacher had been rushed to hospital and had only a few days to live. Michael and Ralf fought for pole position, sharing the front row, before flying off to their mother's bedside, arriving in time to say their goodbyes. Elisabeth passed away at dawn on Sunday.

Ferrari and Williams left it to their drivers to decide whether to go ahead with the grand prix or not. They announced their decision jointly, saying, 'Our mother would have wanted us to race. We will race one another with pain in our hearts,' and indeed they did until Ralf's first pit stop. Then the younger sibling made a slight error, losing ground to his brother and leaving Michael to take his first win of the season, racing the legendary F2002 for the final time. There was no champagne or leaps of joy on the podium. Only hours after the death of his mother, Michael was in mourning with an armband on his sleeve and a heavy heart and he had no wish to celebrate.

'Everyone in the Ferrari team, and I mean everyone, has given me great support,' he said quietly. 'They are very close to me and it has helped me feel better. My mother used to come to the kart track. She loved it when Ralf and I drove on the old track. She loved watching us race. My mother and father always supported us in this, making possible what we have achieved.'

A fortnight later the F2003–GA made its race debut in Spain. The new car had to win, if only to avoid losing marks when compared with the cars that had preceded it since 1999, and Schumacher duly took pole and victory. Barrichello was second in qualifying and set the race's fastest lap on his way to third place. Not much more could have been asked of the car on its debut.

'I'm told the new car is being called a shark, but I think it's more like a goddess because it is really divine. Whatever you want to call it, this GA is still my baby,' said the obviously enamoured Schumacher.

'There is always some apprehension with a new car,' admitted engineer Martinelli, 'even though the last series of tests at Mugello cancelled out any doubt. The new engine is lighter, more compact and has more performance than the old one, but it's the car as a whole that's extraordinary.'

The love affair extended to Austria, where Schumacher continued his winning ways, despite having to deal with flames that engulfed the car during his pit stop on lap twenty-three.

'When I saw the flames, I thought the mechanics reckoned I was feeling the cold and had decided to warm me up,' he joked after the race. 'But really, it wasn't very nice, but the guys did a great job to sort it out. I never doubted their ability. You need to have faith in the team and now, after so many years, I always do. Our mechanics are the best and I trust them one hundred per cent.'

At moments like these, the words of Todt, Brawn, Byrne and Domenicali come to mind on the subject of the current Ferrari being built on the adversities of the past. The mechanics never lost faith in Schumacher, even when he lost two world titles at the final race, and he never lost faith in them, even when an engine expired before the start and a brake failure meant he broke his leg when he crashed off the track. The relationship has strengthened with the passing of time, cemented by the odd game of football in between test sessions, not to mention endless victories, which Michael usually dedicates to every last one of them.

Three wins in a row brought Schumacher to within two points of the championship lead. With some good placings, Raikkonen was able to hang on to the top spot. Criticisms were levelled at the new points system — ten for a win, eight for second, six for third — Montezemolo referring to it as 'taxi driver rules' because it reduced the advantage of winning. With the old points system — ten for a win, six for second, four for third — Schumacher would have been back in the lead by a two-point margin instead of being two points down. 'But these are the rules and although one can talk about them or dislike them, they have to be respected to become world champion,' he commented. It took a further two races for him to top the table after a third place in Monaco and a win in Canada. With Raikkonen second in Monaco, but only sixth in Canada, Schumacher led the series by three points at the halfway stage, while Ferrari headed the constructors' table.

The summer had got off to a good start but it rapidly turned into a nightmare, Schumacher failing to win again from 15 June to 12 September. Bringing a ray of hope to the Ferrari camp, Barrichello won the British Grand Prix at Silverstone in the craziest race of the year. Just like Rubinho's victory at Hockenheim in 2000, this win featured a track invasion.

'I'm sure that Ayrton, on seeing my overtaking moves, would have been standing up to acknowledge them,' Rubino said afterwards. 'I thank God for helping me keep calm and composed at the right moment. Up until a few days ago, no one rated my chances, but now they do. Hockenheim was still the best win, but this one was more exciting and difficult. It was like a kart race where you never know if you're going to damage the car. And there was the overtaking. I made so many passing moves that I can be happy for months. The second one on Raikkonen was the best.'

This was a good year for Barrichello — two wins, three pole positions and he out-qualified Schumacher six times. He saved the day at Silverstone and, even more importantly, he did it again at Suzuka in the final race of the season. Since he came to Maranello, Ferrari has never lost a championship and he deserves some of the credit for that.

'Drivers like Michael come along once every hundred years, but Rubens is a great driver, who has grown and matured a lot over the past few years,' reckons Ross Brawn.

However, Ferrari endured a tough summer. Schumacher managed to hang on to the championship lead, but a seventh place in Germany (a puncture) and eighth in Hungary, where he was even lapped, illustrated the crisis afflicting Maranello. In Germany, if it had not been for the puncture, Schumacher looked set for a podium finish, but the team really touched bottom in Hungary. It was the day that Fernando Alonso became the youngest-ever grand prix winner — one of the few records to have eluded Schumacher.

Between the Hungarian and Italian grands prix, the business of tyres raised its head. Ferrari had spotted that there was something not quite right about those used by the opposition.

'It all began in Budapest,' reveals Ross Brawn. 'It was there that Bridgestone got hold of some photos taken by a Japanese photographer in the paddock, which showed unequivocally that after the race, or at least after they had been used, the Michelin front tyres had an excessively wide contact patch. We had our suspicions but obviously we couldn't take any measurements. We turned to the FIA and to Charlie Whiting. On the basis of his measurements and the photos, it led to us sending the famous letter. We could have made out we were unaware of anything and not advised the FIA and then lodged a protest at the next race but that didn't seem like the right thing to do.'

This is Brawn's technical evaluation of the scenario: 'It all stemmed from the design of the shoulder on the Michelin tyre. On the upper part there's a sort of small ridge that separates the contact area from the outside wall of the tyre. It takes a small amount of use only to wear away the ridge, producing a contact patch that, according to our calculations, is between ten and fifteen per cent wider than when new, and this makes the tyre not conforming to the regulations.

'This explains a lot, such as why Williams hardly ever change their front tyres in a race and why the French company was not able to supply their wider tyres in Monaco. The wider contact patch can produce advantages in terms of weight distribution and better brake balance at the front end. It can help the car change direction better in the corners, and it allows the use of a softer compound with consequent advantages in terms of traction.'

Naturally, Michelin reacted and immediately threatened to take the Ferrari technical director to court, but in the end, they acquiesced and turned up at Monza with different tyres for all their teams.

'The tyres are very important, fundamental in fact,' explains Rory Byrne. 'They can provide the biggest performance gain of any element allowed in the rules today.'

This is why, over the years, Ferrari have intensified their working collaboration with Bridgestone. A more or less exclusive supply agreement effectively means having tyres that are made to measure, but it does require a far heavier testing schedule than would otherwise be the case to make the most of it. Hence it has become commonplace for two Ferrari test teams to run at two and sometimes three tracks at the same time.

During this difficult time, there was no sign of hysteria and no sign of crisis. With analysis in the factory and work on the track, everyone had their role to play and their specific area of responsibility.

'After the races in Germany and Hungary, we tried to understand the causes of what was going on and what steps we should take to remedy the situation,' explains Ross Brawn. 'We identified several areas where we were slightly weak and could do some work. Then, luckily for the final part of the season, we introduced some new aerodynamic solutions and we also changed our approach on tyre development. At one point, we realised we had gone down the wrong road and we went back to the tyres that had helped us win in Austria and at Silverstone. We had very productive test sessions at Monza and Jerez and introduced various other improvements on the car.'

Shell contributed by bringing in new fuel and lubricants and at Monza, a reborn Ferrari took to the track. Monza 2003 brought back memories of Monza 2000. On both occasions, Ferrari had to win. Schumacher still had a one-point lead over Montoya and was two ahead of Raikkonen, but Williams-BMW had slipped ahead in the constructors' table.

'Our strength is that when we find ourselves facing this sort of situation, when we know we cannot afford to get it wrong, we don't panic or get scared. Instead, we push forward in a solid and united fashion,' said Luca Baldisserri, who had handed over the role of Schumacher's race engineer to Chris Dyer in order to concentrate on race strategy planning and acting as a conduit between the factory and the test programme.

Ferrari fought back, as they had learnt to do over the past few years, taking pole position and the win. It had little effect on the championship standings, with Montoya now three points down and Raikkonen seven points in arrears, but it was a sure morale booster as the teams faced the final two-race sprint to the season's end.

'It looked as though it was over for us and now look where we are. We were really motivated and we gave more than a hundred percent and I'm grateful to the lads and the team for what they have done, from the first to the last, even the cleaning lady,' exclaimed a delighted Schumacher. 'The engine people did an amazing job. The engine was a great help and it doesn't matter if this race was the quickest ever in the history of Formula 1. You know I'm not interested in records. What matters is that we have brought home ten points. It is also my fiftieth win with Ferrari and that fills me with pride and satisfaction.

'There are so many reasons why this win is special — the fact I had not won since Canada in mid-June, the fact it might prove to be decisive for the championship, and that I got the win here in Monza to please our fans. Stepping on to the podium here is really an incredible feeling. And let me tell you, the most important thing of all is that we have made the car more competitive, both in qualifying and in the race. No question.'

The new average speed record of 247.585 km/h beat the old record of 242.615 km/h held by Peter Gethin since 1971, and the new top speed record of 368.8 km/h was 4 km/h faster than the speed recorded by Marc Gene's Williams-BMW in practice. Both were reassuring.

'Some performances are the result of a combination of good work from all aspects of the engine-car package,' explained Martinelli. 'We could say it is pleasing, but more important to us engine specialists is that we come to the last, decisive races of the season with an engine improved in performance terms, without losing reliability. The third evolutionary step is to come. The 052 made its debut in Spain, underwent a first step forward at Silverstone and a second in Monza. Of course, for me, as an Italian, winning at Monza is always something extra, but getting through the year without a single engine problem in the races is what really makes us proud.'

The result in Monza owed a great deal to maximum effort from key technical partners such as Bridgestone, Shell and Magneti Marelli, and was very encouraging, especially with the final two races of the season at Indianapolis and Suzuka looming on the horizon.

'I am in the best possible position to tackle these races,' added Schumacher. 'One win and one second place would be enough to guarantee me the world title. But to be really sure, I would prefer to win twice. So, I'm going to test at Jerez for three days rather than having a rest.' Work, work, work was the dominant theme for the next couple of weeks.

However, in Indianapolis the situation got complicated. Schumacher qualified seventh with both Raikkonen, on pole, and Montoya ahead of him.

'I got it wrong at the first two corners, losing a few tenths and that made me push too hard, which meant I lost a bit of time in various other parts,' explained Michael. 'But I'm not too worried because I know we are pretty strong in race trim.'

He had but one aim in the race, namely staying ahead of Montoya, as it seemed that Raikkonen was out of reach. At the most, he could pin his hopes on Barrichello, who was alongside the McLaren on the front row, but the situation changed as soon as the race got under way.

'Thanks to the great job done on the launch control system, I was able to make up for qualifying with a terrific start, which took me straight into the fight,' explained Schumacher, who was already fourth on the opening lap, behind Raikkonen but ahead of Montoya, his most dangerous rival. From then on, the race was, in Schumacher's words, 'mentally very tough, which made it all the more satisfying'.

The race highlighted all Schumacher's best qualities and caused chaos for his main rivals. Montoya made a poor start and then chose the wrong moment to attack Barrichello, for which he was penalised. He lost time in the pits and later spun on his way to sixth place, putting him out of the running for the title. Meanwhile, out in front, Schumacher was making the most of his skills in the rain, having struggled earlier when the track was just damp. For twenty-two laps, he was virtual world champion as Raikkonen was only third behind Frentzen.

'Our tyres were fantastic in the dry, then they struggled a bit when the track was damp before being brilliant when it started to rain hard,' said Schumacher, summing up the situation. 'I just concentrated on staying calm, but at the same time driving hard and aggressively.' When he saw the yellow flags on the horizon, he drove on the limit to get past Panis before reaching the area where he would have been penalised for overtaking under the flags. Then came the moment he found himself behind Montoya, unsure whether or not he should pass him — 'I asked over the radio and luckily I was told that he was a lap down.' At one point, he made the wrong choice of tyres and had to come back into the pits two laps running to switch to rain tyres. It may have been a close shave but, in the end, it was an impressive seventieth grand prix win.

The Indy result meant the title was almost in the bag. With one race remaining, Schumacher and Raikkonen were now the only contenders, although the Finn was trailing by nine points. For Raikkonen to become champion, he had to win at Suzuka and hope that Schumi failed to score a single point.

'It's done? Let's wait and see,' replied Schumacher.

So the talking stopped and the action began. On 2 October, rather than sunning himself, Michael Schumacher was pounding round Mugello. He had dedicated the win in Indianapolis to the lads on the test team who, under the direction of engineer Luigi Mazzola, worked long and hard out of the limelight, and here he was, working with them. This was no ordinary test as he completed no fewer than 129 laps of the Tuscan track, equivalent to around 670 kilometres, or more than two race distances. It underlined the desire to leave nothing to chance and his insistence on looking at every little detail in preparation for the decisive grand prix.

'We are no longer surprised by his dedication,' said Mattia Binotto, his engine specialist, who will become in 2004 Ferrari race engines manager. 'A year ago, just two days after winning the drivers' championship, he was already on testing duty at Mugello at eight in the morning. Anyone else would have got a test driver to stand in for him, but not Michael. He was there on the track as though the championship was yet to be decided. It helps to build team spirit and to boost the motivation of those who work with him.'

For an important test such as this one at Mugello, Ross Brawn and Chris Dyer, the thirty-five year old Australian who took over from Baldisserri at the start of the year as Schumacher's race engineer, also made the trip from Maranello. If Michael is fastidious, so too is Jean Todt.

'One of Todt's talents has been in bringing together all the different cultures that work at Ferrari,' said Baldisserri. 'Italians, English, French and various other nationalities all work in the team without envy, rivalry or any sort of hindrance.'

Todt established work methods and brought stability to the team, with the personnel hardly ever changing. People grow within the team, taking on more important roles as the years go by. It brings security in terms of having a solid base, and ensures the team can remain competitive in the future without going through any more technological black holes.

'The guys who work at Ferrari have more passion than those in other teams,' said Brawn, attempting to sum up the situation. 'It's not the same as in the English or German teams. Here, we feel the passion of the people who live around us. They push us when things are going well and support us when they're going badly. It's incredible. I remember at Benetton, when we got back to the factory after winning the championship, we were met by a group of protesters. They were Damon Hill fans. Here at Maranello, everyone is on our side — and not just at Maranello, judging by the flags we see being waved wherever we go in the world.'

All that remained was to head off to Japan and take an historic championship victory, with just one point needed. But there were surprises in store, specifically the rain that came at the wrong moment, as Schumacher prepared to go out to qualify. As a result, he had to start his quest for the title from fourteenth place on the grid but, luckily for him, Barrichello was on pole and Raikkonen, the one man who could mess up the plans, was only eighth.

The Japanese Grand Prix was not the easiest race of the year. On lap two, Montoya got past Barrichello to take the lead and on lap six, Schumacher broke his front wing in an impetuous move on Sato, forcing him to pit for repairs.

'I lost the nose of my Ferrari because of my own stupidity,' Michael admitted.

The pit work went off perfectly, but he had dropped to twentieth and last once back on the track. Thus began one of the strangest races of his life. He began screaming down the radio, 'Where's Frentzen? What's Coulthard doing? What happened to Montoya? And Sauber, where are they in the constructors' table?' The pits had never heard him so agitated, so Ross Brawn intervened, saying, 'Michael, stay focused on the race.'

With Montoya having retired Barrichello was out in front on a free rein, driving perfectly and keeping second-placed Raikkonen at bay, but it was best not to take any risks. If Barrichello lost first place, Raikkonen would be in the lead and without that single point, Michael would lose the title.

'It was very tough trying to win the race with Rubens and looking after Michael's position,' Brawn said afterwards.

'Michael might have been nervous in the car, but I can tell you, so were we in front of the TV monitors. If I usually check a calculation twice, this time I must have done it ten times,' added Mattia Binotto, the engine man.

With thirteen laps to go, Michael took the eighth place he needed for that point. Then he had to cope with further excitement courtesy of his brother Ralf, who was fighting for the position. As they came up behind Toyota's Cristiano da Matta, the Williams hit the Ferrari from behind. There was no harm done and Michael continued, listening out for the slightest indication that the collision had done some damage. He lived through the final laps with his heart in his mouth, but everything went smoothly and it ended with a win for Barrichello and the drivers' and constructors' championships in the bag.

'It feels very odd celebrating the title with an eighth place,' commented a weary Schumacher after the race. But it did not take much to get this party started for the man who has enjoyed so many since he first donned the red race suit. Before it all began, he found time to add that 'we are one big happy family' — one big happy family by the name of Formula Ferrari.

9 LUCA DI MONTEZEMOLO

The President looks back

A lot was expected of Luca di Montezemolo and the man has delivered. Under his presidency, Ferrari has gone from being an historic team to a sporting legend, winning more than any other team in over fifty years of the Formula 1 World Championship. He has been the heart and mind of a company that needed a firm hand on the tiller, a safe and credible leader, after a run of failures following the death of the company founder in 1988.

For Luca di Montezemolo, a lawyer and now also an honorary engineer, returning to Ferrari was pretty much a homecoming to the place where he grew up and began to make his way in the world. It was difficult to come back at a time of crisis for both the Formula 1 team and the company as a whole but in less than ten years Ferrari was transformed into a benchmark for others, both on the track and in sales terms. The company even took on the task of revitalising another prestigious marque in the shape of Maserati.

Montezemolo achieved this monumental turnaround by putting the right people in place. No magic wands were waved. It came about through work, determination and grit — characteristics that have underscored his life, both private and professional.

Now that winning has become a habit, he can reflect on the last decade or so and try to explain how it all happened, how he went about finding the right formula to get out of the crisis and come out on top. It hasn't been an easy road. Montezemolo had charged Todt with running the Scuderia and always backed that decision. The results took a while to come, but Montezemolo never showed signs of cracking, even in the face of pressure from the Fiat Group. Time proved him right…and how! This is how he tells it:

Ferrari had not won the drivers' title since 1979. Enzo Ferrari spent the last ten years of his life waiting for it to happen and the expectation of this victory had begun to put the future of the company in doubt. There was talk of a switch to becoming just an engine supplier, building engines for Williams or McLaren, and at a time when things were not easy for Fiat, we continued to spend to no effect.

It was not just results that were lacking. There was a continuous turnover of designers at the highest level, and the favourite sport within the company seemed to be blaming others and passing the buck. In 1992 and 1993 we could not even finish in the top three in the constructors' championship.

The first thing to do was to find out why we had not won since 1979 and then organise a response. A ruthless analysis of company know-how revealed a complete lack of experience in three key areas of Formula 1 in the modern era — aerodynamics, new materials and electronics. Italy as a whole was suffering from the lack of an aerospace programme. At Ferrari, we also lacked competence, organisation and team spirit. A complete overhaul was required.

Obviously, something as fundamental as this was not going to reap rewards from one day to the next. With medium and long-term programmes, we expected it would take at least five years to get back on top. The right people had to be found to engender the right culture and work methods. We were coming from a long way back.

It was not difficult to motivate the staff. Everyone was very open to this radical reorganisation. The older ones immediately espoused the new regime and the new recruits brought in a breath of fresh air. We had to go shopping at other teams, but we did it without causing disruption. We wanted a team mentality and sense of rigour, but with Italian passion and spirit. I kept reminding myself that behind exceptional cars, we needed to have exceptional men.

It was important to find the right person to take charge of the Gestione Sportiva. In time, this person would have total authority to rebuild the team, bringing in people to fill the gaps. Jean Todt was our man. He had zero experience of Formula 1, but with the passing months, he became imbued with the Ferrari spirit and culture.

At first, it was not easy for him. We protected him when necessary and provided the right environment for him to do his job and he repaid us with the quality and volume of his work, along with complete loyalty and dedication.

The first sign that we were turning things around, that having touched bottom we were beginning to improve, came with Alesi's second place at Monza in 1993, which was followed by Berger's win in Germany the next year. Michael joined at the right time. Any earlier and the team would not have been ready and any later would have been too late.

Before we started to win, there were times when we dropped our guard. In a previous era, the whole team would have been thrown into turmoil but not now. Even after Schumacher's first win, in Barcelona, some people in Turin were pushing for change because changes were taking place at Fiat, but that would have put us back five years. We held fast and, in the end, I was proved right.

In 1997, we lost the championship fifteen minutes from the chequered flag. Again in 1998, we lost it at the final round, although in my opinion, the key moment that year was the accident between Schumacher and Coulthard at Spa.

In 1999, we tackled almost half the championship without Schumacher, and despite this, with Irvine we were in the running for the title right up to the final race. We did win the constructors' championship, which actually is more important to us as it represents the efforts of both cars.

Some said we did not want to win the drivers' title with Irvine — as though he was racing for another team! For him, we implemented for the first time the use of team orders, slowing Salo in Germany when he was heading for the one and only Formula 1 win of his life. They say Irvine was no Hakkinen and yet he only missed out on the title by two points, a result he never came close to again in his career.

From then on, we started winning. The team was 99 per cent ready. Together we had overcome difficult moments, we were stronger and reinvigorated. In this period was born what I refer to as our dynamic stability, by which I mean that the team does not change but grows from within.

Ferrari is a team with three main characteristics — team spirit, determination when times are hard, linked to humility after victory, and an incredible level of research and innovation in every sector. The research and innovation does not apply just to technology, but also to working practices, organisation and relationships with our partners. Within the company today, we have the managers and engineers of tomorrow. We work on the present while thinking of the future.

Ferrari has broken the record for the number of Formula 1 wins, and this team has also established new records within the company. For instance, never has a driver, or a team principal, been with us for so long, and never have we had a technical caucus — Martinelli, Brawn, Byrne, Simon — stay together for so many years. We are living through an extraordinary, magical time. From the day Schumacher became world champion at Suzuka in 2001, we have not lost. Sooner or later this run must come to an end, but we are aware of having achieved something historic, unique and unrepeatable.

Michael plays an absolutely key role for us. He has an extraordinary ability to drive flat out over a whole race distance, putting in some fantastic laps just before the pit stops. Of course, you must take into account that, these days, the car counts for more than the driver. In the past few years, several world champions were unable to get good results after switching teams. I'm thinking of Damon Hill and Jacques Villeneuve. Without such a strong and united team behind him and without such a competitive and reliable car to drive, even Michael would not have won so much.

He is a great team player and never complains or blames the team, even when there have been technical problems, and this attitude is reciprocated. When he has been in difficulty, the team has always stuck by him. The team never blames the driver and the driver never blames the team.

Barrichello is the best possible team-mate for Schumacher. From the moment he joined, we kept on winning, and he has improved a great deal alongside Michael.

If I had to define Ferrari today I would say it is a unique team and a unique company, an extraordinary mix of passion and technology, with an unrivalled capacity for work and a high level of consistency in the races. I'm sure Enzo Ferrari would be proud of us. Above all else, he taught me two things — never give up and always look ahead. Ferrari today is a tribute to those lessons. The company has shown itself capable of fighting to the end, while at the same time always trying to innovate.

I'm told by various entrepreneurs that we have set a great example, presenting a winning image of Italy on the world stage. That is cause for pride, but it also carries responsibility. Ferrari sells a dream and those who buy the car or follow the team do so partly because we represent that dream. Shortly before Christmas, a doctor in a general hospital in Bologna told me that we even manage to bring a smile to the faces of some of his patients. I had not thought about that before and it is a further impetus to continue down this road.

10 *JEAN TODT'S PERSPECTIVE*

Jean Todt loves modern art, backgammon, wrist watches and, above all, Ferrari. The walls of his light and spacious Fiorano office are covered with photographs of all the team's wins since he was appointed managing director of the racing department in July 1993.

When he arrived, the walls were blank and they stayed that way for quite a while. Then with one win in 1994, another in 1995 and three in 1996, the team gathered momentum and the victories started to accumulate. Now there are sixty-two large red-framed photos on display. They run from a shot of Berger on the Hockenheim podium in 1994 to one of Barrichello winning in Suzuka in 2003. Slap bang in the middle, of course, is Schumacher, with fifty-one Ferrari wins and nine titles secured in five years with the team. There doesn't seem to be space for any more but Todt reckons he 'could manage to fit in another hundred'.

With his abiding belief in hard work, the office must seem like home as he spends long days and often nights there, but he has a house in Paris, another in the French countryside and a rented place in Modena. He also has a son, Nicolas.

Todt was born on 25 February 1946 at Pierrefort, France, into a family of Polish origin. His father was a doctor and Jean achieved various academic honours. Having made his name as a rally co-driver, he at one time headed up the Peugeot motor-sport department, but the phone call from Luca di Montezemolo led to him taking up the Ferrari challenge, which changed his life.

The general scepticism that greeted his arrival has long gone. Everyone has been won over — not by his genial nature but by results. In Formula 1, as in life, that is what counts. The current Ferrari era bears his signature alongside those of Montezemolo, Schumacher, Brawn, Byrne, Martinelli and Barrichello. He is the glue that has held the team together through the hardest of times and he provides the stimulus to push on still harder after the great moments. From the pit wall, and from his office the walls of which bear testament to success, he has led the Italian team that is the envy of the world.

Asked what he had brought to Ferrari that was not there before, he replied, 'Leadership, organisation, working practices, a strong presence and a reference point. Maybe I am a bit too hands-on, but

I always try to solve other people's problems and not just those in the workplace. I'm like that because I want people to be able to concentrate on their job.

'I have changed in some ways, but in others I haven't wanted to, or been able to. I have become more thick-skinned when it comes to fending off criticisms and attacks. I listen more. But you need to be a certain type of person to do this job and I am not the sort to make many concessions although I have had to do so occasionally for the good of the company.'

Interestingly, when asked if he is always at the service of Ferrari, he said, 'In some ways I am a soldier for the company and for all our group.'

But back in 1993, Ferrari presented an alarming picture. In common with all Formula 1 teams, the aim was to start winning as soon as possible. The question was how to do it. Jean Todt takes up the story:

My first official day at work was the Monday after the French Grand Prix at Magny-Cours — two retirements. A great start! I knew then that there was a lot to do. I had already spoken with Lauda, Alesi, Berger, Lombardi and, of course, Montezemolo, so I understood the situation, but I only saw the full picture bit by bit, after I started work. It didn't take much to realise that there were problems. You only had to look at the Formula 1 results sheets to know the score.

Of course, there aren't many Formula 1 teams who race merely to take part. Everyone wants to win but, having said that, Ferrari should have been winning already. On paper, the team had everything they needed to do it, but they were not competitive and that was at the root of the problems.

Ferrari are the greatest race team and company, commanding universal respect, with tradition, culture and the emotion of a country behind them, but everyone has problems, and problems within Ferrari are possibly even greater than elsewhere because we are isolated in a small provincial town.

It was a case of analysing the situation to identify the specific problems and then solving them in order of priority. I soon discovered that what was needed was a revamp of the whole organisation, a new structure. It's like when you go fishing and you have everything ready. The fish come but they do not bite. I confess there were moments when I had my doubts and I asked myself if we would ever manage to win the championship. Yet the people at Ferrari then are the same ones who have taken us to five world championships in a row, and Michael to four consecutive wins.

In fact, the hard times were important for the atmosphere within the company. Difficult moments help you grow. The way in which we were able to deal with them created our sense of unity, strength and spirit. We were always united, never one against the other. We never blamed one another, which was something of a regular occurrence when we had a department based in England. We always made sure we never washed our dirty linen in public.

We started to build on several bases. Take Schumacher, for example. When we took him on, we knew it was a great investment, but we also knew we were taking a big risk. With him on board, we would have only ourselves to blame if we did not win. The other side of the coin was that if we started to win, Schumacher would be given all the credit, but that wasn't important because all that mattered was winning.

At least no one could say we didn't have the driver. His strengths and track record meant there was no doubt on that score.

The turnaround didn't happen just because of Michael, though. Other key changes took place at that time, with Ross and Rory. Enzo Ferrari used to say that the credit for a win had to be divided equally between the car and the driver, but these days the role of the car in the total package represents a much larger percentage than that of the driver. The best driver in the world cannot win with an uncompetitive car. He can give it his best shot, but it won't turn a car into a winning machine if the car is not up to it.

So, can Ferrari win without Schumacher? Well, we saw that at Suzuka with Barrichello in the last race of 2003. Would Ferrari have won so much without Schumacher? I am sure the answer to that is no because he would have exercised his talents with another team. Michael is an extraordinary guy and he has done an exceptional job, but it's well known that I am his biggest fan, so it's not my job to underline that fact. Schumacher has been extraordinary for Ferrari but I believe, and he agrees, that Ferrari has been extraordinary for Schumacher. He has been with us since 1996 and it was said at the time that he would not stay long.

Winning the constructors' championship in 1999 represented the light at the end of the tunnel. It was a bonus — we knew there was still a lot to do. I would have reckoned the drivers' championship, with either Michael or Eddie, would not have been complete without taking the constructors' title.

As it was, we missed out on the drivers' championship and there was a time during 2000 when I felt we were going to miss out again. After Monza, we had to win three of the remaining four races to take the title, our big lead eaten away. Finally to do it was a big relief. People stopped asking me when it would happen and reminding me that we had been trying for twenty-one years.

The calmest year was 2001, when we wrapped up both championships in Budapest. I was so used to suffering at each race that, in those that followed, I forgot we had won it already.

The next year may have looked like a stroll in the park but there was all the fuss after the Austrian Grand Prix. The decision to use team instructions was taken simply because we did not want to run the risk of losing the championship in the final race again. We were like someone who has been starving all his life and is unable to understand that he has finally eaten enough. He always hides a piece of bread in his pocket, forgetting that he can eat caviar every day. Effectively, what we did in Austria was done out of modesty, not out of arrogance.

In 2003 we made more mistakes than in the past and the end of the championship was very reminiscent of the close finish in 2000. The new regulations were brought in as an anti-Ferrari move and we suffered, but there was no witch-hunt — not even in the case of Bridgestone, who had helped us so much in the past. At one stage, Bridgestone had informed us that there was something about our rivals' tyres that did not comply with the regulations and we asked the FIA for clarification. We could not close our eyes to it, pretending nothing was going on. We were made aware that someone was doing something illegal and we brought it to the attention of the Federation.

Looking back, you can't help remembering the best and the worst times. Among all the great days, the best was probably when we took that first world championship win in Suzuka. One of the worst was when Michael had his accident at Silverstone in 1999. The health of a driver and the life of a human being, whomever it might be, are more important than winning or losing a championship. Jerez in 1997 and Spa in 1998 were pretty bad days, and the accident with Coulthard that cost us the championship was not the happiest of times. We've lost several races we deserved to win and won a few that we did not — I'm thinking of Spain in 2001 when Hakkinen stopped on the last lap — but overall we have been tremendously successful.

Having the right people in the right positions and the means to work are the keys. Nothing is missing. We don't have infinite resources, but we have made the best use of what we have. With great commercial and technical partners, and the backing of our shareholders, we have a great company that can be an example to everyone.

Now, in 2004, I would say that Ferrari is a jewel in the world of the motor industry. We have achieved incredible results, especially when you consider the level of the opposition on a sporting and industrial front. Importantly, we have established good relationships within the industry, and there is mutual respect.

We have won much more than I expected but the will to go on is ever present. I have never worked so hard in all my life. It's not a question of motivation but simply a professional conscience and the desire to leave no stone unturned. I cannot manage to observe from a distance.

At Ferrari, I believe we have a duty to work not only for today and for tomorrow, but also for the mid and long-term. We are preparing for the future. It is one of our responsibilities. Today's major players within the team want to ensure Ferrari is competitive long after they have gone. That's for sure.

...scari (5th), Dorino ...ymond Sommer (13th),

...nted 60° V12, Silumin ... head, screw-fitted ...nder spacing 108mm, ...nsmission: rear-wheel ...clutch, 4-speed gearbox ...with ZF limited-slip ...is: tubular with elliptical

section side members and tubular cross members. Brakes: finned drums all round, separate master hydraulic cylinders. Length 3,937mm; width 1,428mm; height 960mm; kerb weight (with water and oil) 720kg

Ascari celebrates secon... Italian Grand Prix

1954

Drivers: José Froilan Gonzalez (2nd), Mike Hawthorn (3rd), Maurice Trintignant (4th), Giuseppe Farina (8th), Robert Manzon (15th), Alberto Ascari, Piero Taruffi.
GP won: 2 — Great Britain 17 July, Spain 24 October
553 F1
Engine: type 106, front-mounted, naturally aspirated in-line 4, light alloy cylinder block and head, 138mm connecting rods, steel cylinder liners, water cooled.
Transmission: rear-wheel drive, multi-plate clutch, 4-speed gearbox + reverse in unit with limited-slip differential. Chassis: type 553, tubular steel. Brakes: hydraulic finned drums all round, separate master cylinder for front and rear axle. Length 3,988mm; width 1,427mm; height 1020mm; kerb weight (with water and oil) 590kg

Hawthorn leads Trintignant in the Spanish Grand Prix

1955

Drivers: Maurice Trintignant (4th), Giuseppe Farina (5th), José Froilan Gonzalez (2nd), Umberto Maglioli (21st), Eugenio Castellotti, Paul Frere, Mike Hawthorn, Piero Taruffi.
GP won: 1 — Monaco 22 May
625 F1
Engine: type 107, front-mounted in-line 4, light alloy cylinder block and head, inserted cylinder liners, 5-bearing crankshaft, water cooled. Transmission: rear-wheel drive, multi-plate clutch, 4-speed gearbox+reverse in unit with limited-slip differential. Chassis: type 500, tubular steel. Brakes: hydraulic finned drums all round, separate master cylinder for front and rear axle. Length 3,988mm; width 1,427mm; height 1020mm; kerb weight (with water and oil) 600kg

Trintignant with the Monaco Grand Prix winner's trophy

1956

Drivers: Juan Manuel Fangio (1st), Peter Collins (3rd), Eugenio Castellotti (6th), Luigi Musso (11th), Alfonso De Portago (15th), Olivier Gendebien (19th), Paul Frere, Andre Pilette, Wolfgang von Trips.
GP won: 5 — Argentina 22 January, Belgium 3 June, France 1 July, Great Britain 14 July, Germany 5 August
D50
Engine: 90° V8, aspirated, front-mounted, light alloy cylinder block and head, press-fitted cast-iron cylinder liners, 135mm connecting rods, water cooled. Transmission: rear-wheel drive, dry twin-plate clutch, rear transverse 5-speed gearbox + reverse, in unit with limited-slip differential. Chassis: steel tube structure. Brakes: drums on all four wheels with hydraulic control. Length 3,850mm; width 1,448mm; height 962mm; kerb weight (with water and oil) 640kg

Fangio at the Monaco Grand Prix

1957

Drivers: Luigi Musso (3rd), Mike Hawthorn (4th), Peter Collins (8th), Maurice Trintignant (12th), Wolfgang von Trips (14th), Alfonso de Portago (20th), José Froilan Gonzalez (20th), José Froilan Gonzalez (20th), Eugenio Castellotti, Cesare Perdisa.
GP won: 0
801 F1
Engine: front-mounted, aspirated, 90° V8, light alloy cylinder block and head, press-fitted cast-iron cylinder liners, 135mm connecting rods, water cooled. Transmission: rear-wheel drive, dry twin-plate clutch, rear transverse 5-speed gearbox + reverse, in unit with limited-slip differential. Chassis: type F1 8CL, steel tube structure. Brakes: bimetallic finned drums on all four wheels, hydraulic control. Length 3,850mm; width 1,448mm; height 962mm; kerb weight (with water and oil) 650kg

Musso at the Pescara Grand Prix

1958

Constructors' Championship (first year held): 2nd

Drivers: Mike Hawthorn (1st), Peter Collins (5th), Luigi Musso (7th), Phil Hill (10th), Wolfgang von Trips (10th), Olivier Gendebien.

GP won: 2 — France 6 July, Great Britain 19 July

246 F1

Engine: type 143, front longitudinally mounted 65° V6, light alloy cylinder block and head, cast-iron wet liners, 132mm connecting rods, water cooled. Transmission: rear-wheel drive, multi-plate clutch, 523 4-speed gearbox + reverse, mounted transversally in unit with ZF limited-slip differential. Chassis: type 528, composed of two main elliptic tubes and other small tubes to form a light, rigid structure. Brakes: front — hydraulic drums with helical fins, 350x48mm; rear — hydraulic drums with helical fins, 300x50mm. Length 4,030mm; width 1,500mm; height 980mm; kerb weight (with water and oil) 560kg

Collins winning the British Grand Prix, Silverstone

1959

Constructors' Championship: 2nd

Drivers: Tony Brooks (2nd), Phil Hill (4th), Dan Gurney (7th), Olivier Gendebien (15th), Cliff Allison (17th), Jean Behra (17th), Wolfgang von Trips.

GP won: 2 — France 5 July, Germany 2 August

256 F1

Engine: type 155/59, front-mounted 65° V6, light alloy cylinder block and head, cast-iron wet liners, 135mm connecting rods, water cooled. Transmission: rear-wheel drive, dry multi-plate hydraulic clutch, 528/B 5-speed gearbox + reverse, in unit with limited-slip differential. Chassis: type 528/B, tubular steel spaceframe. Brakes: hydraulic Dunlop discs on all four wheels. Length 4,030mm; width 1,500mm; height 980mm; kerb weight (with water and oil) 560kg

Brooks and Hill finish first and second in the French Grand Prix

1960

Constructors' Championship: 3rd

Drivers: Phil Hill (5th), Wolfgang von Trips (6th), Richie Ginther (8th), Cliff Allison (12th), Willy Mairesse (15th), José Froilan Gonzalez.

GP won: 1 — Italy 4 September

256 F1

Engine: type 155/59, front-mounted 65° V6, light alloy cylinder block and head, cast-iron wet liners, 135mm connecting rods, water cooled. Transmission: rear-wheel drive, dry multi-plate hydraulic clutch, 528/B 5-speed gearbox + reverse, in unit with limited-slip differential. Chassis: type 528/B, tubular steel spaceframe. Brakes: hydraulic Dunlop discs on all four wheels. Length 4,030mm; width 1,500mm; height 980mm; kerb weight (with water and oil) 560kg

Hill having won the Italian Grand Prix

1961

Constructors' Championship: 1st

Drivers: Phil Hill (1st), Wolfgang von Trips (2nd), Richie Ginther (5th), Giancarlo Baghetti (9th), Olivier Gendebien, Willy Mairesse, Ricardo Rodriguez.

GP won: 5 — Holland 22 May, Belgium 18 June, France 2 July, Great Britain 15 July, Italy 10 September

156 F1

Engine: type 178, rear-mounted 120 ° V6, light alloy cylinder block and heads, aluminium wet liners, 126mm connecting rods, water cooled. Transmission: rear-wheel drive, dry multi-plate clutch behind gearbox, damper springs, 543/C overhanging longitudinal 5-speed gearbox + reverse, plunger-type limited-slip differential. Chassis: type 543/C, tubular steel. Brakes: Dunlop discs and callipers, inboard at rear on the transmission housing, independent circuits with twin pump. Length 4,060mm; width 1,400mm; height 1,000mm; kerb weight (with water and oil) 420kg

The Ferrari race director Ugo Chiti with the team at the Orlando Grand Prix

1962

Constructors' Championship: 5th
Drivers: Phil Hill (6th), Giancarlo Baghetti (11th), Ricardo Rodriguez (12th), Lorenzo Bandini (12th), Willy Mairesse (14th).
GP won: 0
156 F1
Engine: type 178, rear-mounted 120° V6, light alloy cylinder block and heads, aluminium wet liners, 126mm connecting rods, water cooled. Transmission: rear-wheel drive, dry multi-plate clutch behind gearbox, damper springs, 543/C overhanging longitudinal 5-speed gearbox + reverse, plunger-type limited-slip differential. Chassis: type 543/C, tubular steel. Brakes: Dunlop discs and callipers, inboard at rear on the transmission housing, independent circuits with twin pump. Length 4,060mm; width 1,400mm; height 1,000mm; kerb weight (with water and oil) 420kg

Hill at the Monaco Grand Prix

1963

Constructors' Championship: 4th
Drivers: John Surtees (4th), Lorenzo Bandini (9th), Ludovico Scarfiotti (15th), Willy Mairesse.
GP won: 1 — Germany 4 August
156 F1-63
Engine: type 178, rear-mounted 120° V6, light alloy cylinder block and heads, cast-iron wet liners, 126mm connecting rods, water cooled. Transmission: rear-wheel drive, dry multi-plate clutch behind 565/C overhanging longitudinal 6-speed gearbox + reverse, plunger-type limited-slip differential. Chassis: type 565/C, tubular steel. Brakes: Dunlop discs and callipers, inboard at rear on the transmission housing, independent hydraulic circuits. Length 3,900mm; width 790mm; height 810mm; kerb weight (with water and oil) 460kg

Surtees at the South African Grand Prix

1964

Constructors' Championship: 1st
Drivers: John Surtees (1st), Lorenzo Bandini (4th), Ludovico Scarfiotti.
GP won: 3 — Germany 2 August, Austria 23 August, Italy 6 September
158 F1
Engine: type 205/B, rear-mounted 90° V8, light alloy cylinder block and heads, cast-iron cylinder liners, 5-bearing crankshaft, 120mm connecting rods, water cooled. Transmission: rear-wheel drive, dry multi-plate clutch, 579 overhanging longitudinal 5-speed gearbox + reverse, plunger-type limited-slip differential. Chassis: type 579, aluminium panels with double wall riveted to a tubular steel structure to form a stress-bearing semi-monocoque. Brakes: Dunlop discs and callipers, inboard at rear on the differential housing, independent circuits with double pump. Length 3,950mm; width 697mm; height 768mm; kerb weight (with water and oil) 468kg

Scarfiotti's car at the Italian Grand Prix, Monza

1965

Constructors' Championship: 4th
Drivers: John Surtees (5th), Lorenzo Bandini (6th), Ludovico Scarfiotti, Nino Vaccarella.
GP won: 0
512 F1
Engine: type 207, rear-mounted 180° V12, light alloy cylinder block and head, cast-iron wet liners, 110mm connecting rods, water cooled. Transmission: rear-wheel drive, multi-plate clutch, 12C overhanging longitudinal 5-speed gearbox + reverse, plunger-type limited-slip differential. Chassis: type 582, monocoque, aluminium panels with double wall riveted to a tubular steel structure. Brakes: Dunlop discs and callipers mounted inboard on rear axle housing, independent hydraulic circuits with double pump. Length 3,950mm; width 697mm; height 768mm; kerb weight (with water and oil) 490kg

The British Grand Prix, Silverstone — Bandini retires

1966
Constructors' Championship: 2nd
Drivers: John Surtees (2nd), Lorenzo
Bandini (8th), Mike Parkes (8th), Ludovico
Scarfiotti (10th).
GP won: 2 — Belgium 12 June, Italy 4
September
312 F1-1966
Engine: type 218, rear-mounted 60° V12
(derived from 216), light alloy cylinder
block and head, special cast-iron wet
liners, 126mm connecting rods, water
cooled. Transmission: rear-wheel drive,
Borg&Beck multi-plate clutch, 589 rear
longitudinal overhanging 5-speed gearbox
+ reverse, plunger-type limited-slip
differential. Chassis: type 589,
monocoque, aluminium panels in double
wall riveted to a tubular steel structure.
Brakes: Girling discs and callipers,
inboard at rear on differential housing,
independent hydraulic circuits, two
pumps. Length 3,830mm; width 760mm;
height 870mm; kerb weight (with water
and oil) 548kg

*Mechanics prepare Surtees'
car at the Monaco Grand Prix*

1967
Constructors' Championship: 4th
Drivers: Chris Amon (4th), Mike Parkes
(16th), Ludovico Scarfiotti (19th), Lorenzo
Bandini, Jonathan Williams.
GP won: 0
312 F1-1967
Engine: type 242, rear-mounted 60° V12
(derived from 237), light alloy cylinder
block and head, special cast-iron wet
liners, 112mm connecting rods, water
cooled. Transmission: rear-wheel drive,
Borg&Beck multi-plate clutch, 606 rear
longitudinal overhanging 5-speed gearbox
+ reverse, plunger-type limited-slip
differential. Chassis: Type 606,
monocoque, aluminium panels in double
wall riveted to a tubular steel structure.
Brakes: Girling discs and callipers, inboard
at rear on differential housing,
independent hydraulic circuits. Length
3,970mm; width 720mm; height 885mm;
kerb weight (with water and oil) 548kg

Orlando Grand Prix

1968
Constructors' Championship: 4th
Drivers: Jacky Ickx (4th), Chris Amon
(10th), Derek Bell, Andrea de Adamich.
GP won: 1 — France 7 July
312 F1-68
Engine: type 242/C, rear-mounted 60°
V12, light alloy cylinder block and head,
special cast-iron wet liners, 112mm
connecting rods, water cooled.
Transmission: rear-wheel drive,
Borg&Beck multi-plate clutch, 606 L rear
longitudinal overhanging 5-speed gearbox
+ reverse, ZF plunger-type limited-slip
differential. Chassis: type 606B,
monocoque, aluminium panels in double
wall riveted to tubular steel structure.
Brakes: Girling discs and callipers, inboard
at rear on differential housing,
independent hydraulic circuits. Length
4,050mm; width 720mm; height 850mm;
kerb weight (with water and oil) 507kg

*Ickx at the French Grand
Prix, Rouen*

1969
Constructors' Championship: 5th
Drivers: Chris Amon (12th), Pedro
Rodriguez (13th).
GP won: 0
312 F1-69
Engine: type 255/C, rear-mounted 60°
V12, light alloy cylinder block and head,
special cast-iron wet liners, 116mm
connecting rods, lateral exhausts, water
cooled. Transmission: rear-wheel drive,
Borg&Beck multi-plate clutch, 609 rear
longitudinal overhanging 5-speed gearbox
+ reverse, ZF plunger-type limited-slip
differential. Chassis: type 609,
monocoque, aluminium panels in double
wall riveted to tubular steel structure.
Brakes: Girling discs and callipers, inboard
at rear on differential housing,
independent hydraulic circuits. Length
4,060mm; width 738mm; height 910mm;
kerb weight (with water and oil) 530kg

Amon at the French Grand Prix

1970

Constructors' Championship: 2nd
Drivers: Jacky Ickx (2nd), Clay Regazzoni (3rd), Ignazio Giunti (17th).
GP won: 4 — Austria 16 August, Italy 6 September, Canada 20 September, Mexico 25 October
312 B
Engine: type 001, rear-mounted 180° V12, light alloy cylinder block and head, aluminium wet liners, 112mm connecting rods, water cooled. Transmission: rear-wheel drive, Borg&Beck multi-plate clutch,

001 rear longitudinal overhanging 5-speed gearbox + reverse, in unit with multi-plate limited-slip differential. Chassis: type 001, monocoque body, aluminium panels riveted on a tubular steel structure, partially stress-bearing engine. Brakes: outboard Girling discs and callipers, separate adjustable hydraulic circuits on the two axles. Length 4,020mm; width 742mm; height 956mm; kerb weight (with water and oil) 551kg

Ickx with Forghieri at the Monaco Grand Prix

1971

Constructors' Championship: 3rd
Drivers: Jacky Ickx (4th), Clay Regazzoni (7th), Mario Andretti (8th).
GP won: 2 — South Africa 6 March, Holland 20 June
312 B2
Engine: type 001/1, rear-mounted 180° V12 (derived from the 001), light alloy cylinder block and head, aluminium wet liners, 112mm connecting rods, water cooled. Transmission: rear-wheel drive, Borg&Beck multi-plate clutch, 621 rear

longitudinal overhanging 5-speed gearbox + reverse, multi-plate limited-slip differential. Chassis: type 621/A, monocoque, aluminium panels riveted on a tubular steel structure, partially stress-bearing engine. Brakes: Lockheed discs and callipers, inboard at rear, separate adjustable hydraulic circuits on the two axles. Length 3,850mm; width 750mm; height 900mm; kerb weight (with water and oil) 560kg

Ickx at the Spanish Grand Prix

1972

Constructors' Championship: 4th
Drivers: Jacky Ickx (4th), Clay Regazzoni (6th), Mario Andretti (12th), Nanni Galli, Arturo Merzario.
GP won:1 — Germany 30 July
312 B2
Engine: type 001/1, rear-mounted 180° V12 (derived from the 001), light alloy cylinder block and head, aluminium wet liners, 112mm connecting rods, water cooled. Transmission: rear-wheel drive, Borg&Beck multi-plate clutch, 621 rear

longitudinal overhanging 5-speed gearbox + reverse, multi-plate limited-slip differential. Chassis: type 621/A, monocoque body, aluminium panels riveted on a tubular steel structure, partially stress-bearing engine. Brakes: Lockheed discs and callipers, inboard at rear, separate adjustable hydraulic circuits on the two axles. Length 3,850mm; width 750mm; height 900mm; kerb weight (with water and oil) 560kg

Andretti trails Regazzoni at the Spanish Grand Prix

1973

Constructors' Championship: 6th
Drivers: Jacky Ickx (9th), Arturo Merzario (12th).
GP won: 0
312 B3-1973
Engine: type 001/1, rear-mounted 180° V12 (derived from the 001/1), light alloy cylinder block and head, aluminium wet cylinder liners, 112mm connecting rods, water cooled. Transmission: rear-wheel drive, Borg&Beck multi-plate clutch, 628 rear longitudinal overhanging 5-speed

gearbox + reverse, in unit with limited-slip differential. Chassis: type 628, monocoque in boxed sheet aluminium. Brakes: Lockheed discs and callipers, inboard at rear, separate hydraulic circuits, adjustable on the two axles. Length 4,335mm; width 2,056mm; height 900mm; kerb weight (with water and oil) 578kg

Ickx at the French Grand Prix

1974
Constructors' Championship: 2nd
Drivers: Clay Regazzoni (2nd), Niki Lauda (4th).
GP won: 3 – Spain 28 April, Holland 23 June, Germany 4 August
312 B3-1974
Engine: type 001/12, rear-mounted 180° V12, light alloy cylinder block and heads, cast-iron wet liners, 112mm connecting rods, water cooled. Transmission: rear-wheel drive, Borg&Beck multi-plate clutch, 627 longitudinal overhanging 5-speed gearbox + reverse, in unit with limited-slip differential. Chassis: type 628/B, monocoque, aluminium panels riveted to a tubular steel structure. Brakes: discs with Lockheed callipers, outboard at front, inboard at rear, independent hydraulic circuits on the two axles. Length 4,335mm; width 2,056mm; height 900mm; kerb weight (with water and oil) 582kg

Lauda wins the Spanish Grand Prix

1975
Constructors' Championship: 1st
Drivers: Niki Lauda (1st), Clay Regazzoni (5th).
GP won: 6 – Monaco 11 May, Belgium 25 May, Sweden 8 June, France 6 July, Italy 7 September, USA 5 October
312 T
Engine: type 015, rear-mounted 180° V12, light alloy cylinder block and head, aluminium wet liners, 112mm connecting rods, water cooled. Transmission: rear-wheel drive, Borg&Beck multi-plate clutch, 015 transverse-mounted inboard 5-speed gearbox + reverse, friction-plate limited-slip differential. Chassis: type 015, monocoque, aluminium panels riveted to rectangular section tubular steel structure with boxed supports. Brakes: discs and Lockheed callipers, inboard at rear. Length 4,143mm; width 2,030mm; height 1,275mm; kerb weight (with water and oil) 575kg

Regazzoni and Lauda before the Spanish Grand Prix

1976
Constructors' Championship: 1st
Drivers: Niki Lauda (2nd), Clay Regazzoni (5th), Carlos Reutemann (16th).
GP won: 6 – Brazil 25 January, South Africa 6 March, USA West 28 March, Belgium 16 May, Monaco 30 May, Great Britain 18 July
312 T2
Engine: type 015, rear-mounted 180° V12, light alloy cylinder block and head, aluminium wet liners, 112mm connecting rods, water cooled. Transmission: rear-wheel drive, Borg&Beck multi-plate clutch, 015 5-speed gearbox + reverse, transverse in unit with friction-plate limited-slip differential. Chassis: type 629, monocoque with aluminium panels riveted to variable section light alloy structure. Brakes: Brembo discs, Lockheed callipers, inboard at rear. Length 4,316mm; width 1,930mm; height 1,020mm; kerb weight (with water and oil) 575kg

Lauda at the Spanish Grand Prix

1977
Constructors' Championship: 1st
Drivers: Niki Lauda (1st), Carlos Reutemann (4th), Gilles Villeneuve.
GP won: 4 – Brazil 23 January, South Africa 5 March, Germany 31 July, Holland 28 August
312 T2
Engine: type 015, rear-mounted 180° V12, light alloy cylinder block and head, aluminium wet liners, 112mm connecting rods, water cooled. Transmission: rear-wheel drive, Borg&Beck multi-plate clutch, 015 5-speed gearbox + reverse, transverse in unit with friction-plate limited-slip differential. Chassis: type 029, monocoque with aluminium panels riveted to variable section light alloy structure. Brakes: Brembo discs, Lockheed callipers, inboard at rear. Length 4,316mm; width 1,930mm; height 1,020mm; kerb weight (with water and oil) 575kg

Reutemann takes the chequered flag in third place in the Austrian Grand Prix

1978

Constructors' Championship: 2nd
Drivers: Carlos Reutemann (3rd), Gilles Villeneuve (9th).
GP won: 5 — Brazil 29 January, USA West 2 April, Great Britain 16 July, USA 1 October, Canada 8 October
312 T3
Engine: type 015, rear-mounted 180° V12, light alloy cylinder block and head, aluminium wet liners, 112mm connecting rods, water cooled. Transmission: rear-wheel drive, Borg&Beck multi-plate clutch,

020 5-speed gearbox + reverse, transverse in unit with limited-slip differential. Chassis: type 020, monocoque, aluminium panels riveted to variable section light alloy structure and cast light alloy supports. Brakes: Lockheed callipers and Brembo ventilated cast-iron discs, inboard at rear on differential. Length 4,250mm; width 2,130mm; height 1,010mm; kerb weight (with water and oil) 580kg

Reutemann winning the British Grand Prix

1979

Constructors' Championship: 1st
Drivers: Jody Scheckter (1st), Gilles Villeneuve (2nd).
GP won: 6 — South Africa 3 March, USA West 8 April, Belgium 13 May, Monaco 27 May, Italy 9 September, USA 7 October
312 T4
Engine: type 015, rear-mounted 180° V12, light alloy cylinder block and head, aluminium wet liners, 112mm connecting rods, water cooled. Transmission: rear-wheel drive, Borg&Beck multi-plate clutch,

022 5-speed gearbox + reverse, transverse in unit with limited-slip differential. Chassis: type 022, monocoque, aluminium panels riveted to variable section light alloy structure and light alloy supports. Brakes: Lockheed callipers and Brembo ventilated cast-iron discs, inboard on differential at rear. Length 4,460mm; width 2,120mm; height 1,010mm; kerb weight (with water and oil) 590kg

Villeneuve and Scheckter on the podium, first and second in the USA West Grand Prix, Long Beach

1980

Constructors' Championship: 10th
Drivers: Gilles Villeneuve (10th), Jody Scheckter (19th).
GP won: 0
312 T5
Engine: type 015, rear-mounted 180° V12, light alloy cylinder block and head, aluminium wet liners, 112mm connecting rods, water cooled. Transmission: rear-wheel drive, multi-plate clutch, 022 5- or 6-speed gearbox + reverse, transverse in unit with limited-slip differential. Chassis:

type 023, monocoque, aluminium panels riveted to variable section light alloy structure and cast alloy supports. Brakes: Brembo ventilated cast-iron discs, Lockheed callipers. Length 4,530mm; width 2,120mm; height 1,020mm; kerb weight (with water and oil) 595kg

Villeneuve on his way to fifth place in the Monaco Grand Prix

1981

Constructors' Championship: 5th
Drivers: Gilles Villeneuve (7th), Didier Pironi (13th).
GP won: 2 — Monaco 31 May, Spain 21 June
126 CK
Engine: type 021, rear-mounted 120° V6, light alloy cylinder block and heads, aluminium wet liners, water cooled. Transmission: rear-wheel drive, multi-plate clutch, 021 5-speed gearbox + reverse, transverse in unit with limited-slip

differential. Chassis: type 024, monocoque, aluminium panels riveted to a variable section light alloy structure and cast alloy supports. Brakes: Brembo ventilated cast-iron discs on wheels, Lockheed callipers. Length 4,468mm; width 2,110mm; height 1,025mm; kerb weight (with water and oil) 600kg

Pironi at the British Grand Prix

1982

Constructors' Championship: 1st
Drivers: Didier Pironi (2nd), Patrick
Tambay (7th), Gilles Villeneuve (15th),
Mario Andretti (19th).
GP won: 3 — San Marino 25 April, Holland
3 July, Germany 8 August
126 C2
Engine: type 021, rear-mounted 120° V6,
light alloy cylinder block and heads,
aluminium wet liners, water cooled.
Transmission: rear-wheel drive, multi-plate
clutch, reduced with 025 5-speed gearbox
+ reverse, transverse in unit with ZF
limited-slip friction-plates differential.
Chassis: type 631, monocoque, mixed
aluminium/carbon-fibre honeycomb and
Hexcel base material. Brakes: ventilated
cast-iron discs all round, Brembo
aluminium callipers. Length 4,333mm;
width 2,110mm; height 1,025mm; kerb
weight (with water and oil) 595kg

Pironi at the Belgian Grand Prix

1983

Constructors' Championship: 1st
Drivers: René Arnoux (3rd), Patrick
Tambay (4th).
GP won: 4 — San Marino 1 May, Canada
12 June, Germany 7 August, Holland
28 August
126 C3
Engine: type 021, rear-mounted 120° V6,
light alloy cylinder block and heads,
aluminium wet liners, water cooled.
Transmission: rear-wheel drive, multi-plate
clutch, 025 5- or 6-speed gearbox +
reverse, transverse in unit with ZF limited-
slip friction-plate differential. Chassis: type
632, monocoque, two Kevlar and carbon-
fibre composite shells bonded and bolted
together. Brakes: ventilated cast-iron discs
all round, Brembo aluminium callipers.
Length 4,130mm; width 2,110mm; height
1,025mm; kerb weight (with water and
oil) 552kg

Tambay wins the San Marino Grand Prix

1984

Constructors' Championship: 2nd
Drivers: Michele Alboreto (4th), René
Arnoux (6th).
GP won: 1 — Belgium 29 April
126 C4
Engine: type 031, rear-mounted 120° V6,
light alloy cylinder block and heads,
aluminium wet liners, water cooled.
Transmission: rear-wheel drive, multi-plate
clutch, 633 5-speed gearbox + reverse,
transverse in unit with limited-slip
differential. Chassis: type 633 monocoque
in Kevlar carbon-fibre composite. Brakes:
ventilated cast-iron discs, Brembo 4-piston
cast aluminium callipers. Length 4,115mm;
width 2,125mm; height 1,080mm; kerb
weight (with water and oil) 540kg

Alboreto winning the Belgian Grand Prix

1985

Constructors' Championship: 2nd
Drivers: Michele Alboreto (2nd), Stefan
Johansson (7th), René Arnoux (17th).
GP won: 2 — Canada 16 June, Germany
4 August
156-85
Engine: type 031, rear-mounted 120° V6,
light alloy cylinder block and heads,
aluminium wet liners, water cooled.
Transmission: rear-wheel drive, multi-plate
clutch, 635 5-speed gearbox + reverse,
transverse-mounted incorporating the
engine oil tank, ZF limited-slip differential.
Chassis: new CAD-designed type 635
monocoque, honeycomb composite with
carbon-fibre and Kevlar. Brakes: carbon-
fibre discs, 4-pot Brembo callipers on all
four wheels. Length 4,292mm; width
2,135mm; height 1,080mm; kerb weight
(with water and oil) 548kg

*Alboreto and Johansson lead the
German Grand Prix*

1986

Constructors' Championship: 4th
Drivers: Stefan Johansson (5th), Michele
Alboreto (8th).
GP won: 0
F1-86
Engine: type 032, rear-mounted 120° V6,
light alloy cylinder block and heads,
aluminium wet liners, water cooled.
Transmission: rear-wheel drive, multi-plate
clutch, 636 5-speed gearbox + reverse, in
unit with limited-slip differential. Chassis:
type 636, monocoque in carbon-fibre
honeycomb and Kevlar composite.
Brakes: ventilated carbon discs on all
four wheels, Ferrari built callipers. Length
4,296mm; width 2,120mm; height 920mm;
kerb weight (with water and oil) 548kg,
max. 576kg

Johansson at the French Grand Prix

1987

Constructors' Championship: 4th
Drivers: Gerhard Berger (5th), Michele
Alboreto (7th).
GP won: 2 – Japan 1 November, Australia
15 November
F1-87
Engine: type 033/D, rear-mounted 90°
V6, cast-iron cylinder block without wet
liners, light alloy head, water cooled.
Transmission: rear-wheel drive, multi-plate
clutch, 638 rear longitudinal overhanging
6-speed gearbox + reverse, ZF limited-slip
differential. Chassis: type 638, carbon-
fibre honeycomb and Kevlar composite
honeycomb monocoque. Brakes: ventilated
carbon discs on all four wheels, Brembo
4-pot callipers. Length 4,280mm; width
2,120mm; height 1,000mm; kerb weight
(with water and oil) 542kg

Berger wins the Australian Grand Prix

1988

Constructors' Championship: 2nd
Drivers: Gerhard Berger (3rd), Michele
Alboreto (5th).
GP won: 1 – Italy 11 September
F1-87/88
Engine: type 033/E, rear-mounted 90°
V6, special cast-iron cylinder block without
wet liners, light alloy head, water cooled.
Transmission: rear-wheel drive, multi-plate
carbon-fibre clutch, 638 longitudinal
overhanging mechanical 6-speed gearbox
+ reverse, ZF limited-slip differential.
Chassis: type 638/A, honeycomb
carbon-fibre and Kevlar composite.
Brakes: ventilated carbon-fibre discs on
all four wheels, Brembo callipers. Length
4,280mm; width 2,120mm; height
1,000mm; kerb weight (with water and
oil) 542kg

*Berger and Alboreto, first and second in
the Italian Grand Prix, Monza*

1989

Constructors' Championship: 3rd
Drivers: Nigel Mansell (4th), Gerhard
Berger (7th).
GP won: 3 – Brazil 26 March, Hungary 13
August, Portugal 24 September
F1-89
Engine: type 035/5, rear-mounted 65°
V12, special cast-iron cylinder block
without wet liners, light alloy head, 112mm
connecting rods, water cooled.
Transmission: rear-wheel drive, three-plate
steel clutch with mechanical and
automatic control, 640/A longitudinal
overhanging 7-speed gearbox + reverse,
semi-automatic with electronic
management. Chassis: type 640, single-
piece monocoque, carbon-fibre and Kevlar
honeycomb. Brakes: ventilated carbon-
fibre discs and one-piece Brembo callipers
on all four wheels. Length 4,400mm; width
2,130mm; height 950mm; kerb weight
(with water and oil) 505kg

Mansell at the San Marino Grand Prix

1990

Constructors' Championship: 2nd
Drivers: Alain Prost (2nd), Nigel Mansell (5th).
GP won: 6 – Brazil 25 March, Mexico 24 June, France 8 July, Great Britain 15 July, Portugal 23 September, Spain 30 September
F1-90
Engine: type 036, rear-mounted 65° V12, cast-iron cylinder block without wet liners, light alloy head, 112mm connecting rods, water cooled. Transmission: rear-wheel drive, three-plate carbon clutch with mechanical and automatic control, 641 longitudinal overhanging 7-speed gearbox + reverse, semi-automatic with electronic management. Chassis: type 641 monocoque in carbon-fibre and Kevlar honeycomb. Brakes: ventilated carbon-fibre discs, Brembo one-piece callipers on all four wheels. Length 4,460mm; width 2,130mm; height 1,000mm; kerb weight (with water and oil) 503kg

Prost winning the British Grand Prix, Silverstone

1991

Constructors' Championship: 3rd
Drivers: Alain Prost (5th), Jean Alesi (7th), Gianni Morbidelli (24th).
GP won: 0
F1-91
Engine: rear-mounted 60° V12, special cast-iron cylinder block without wet liners, light alloy head, water cooled.
Transmission: rear-wheel drive, three-plate carbon clutch with mechanical and automatic control, rear longitudinal overhanging 7-speed gearbox + reverse, automatic with electronic management, ZF limited-slip differential. Chassis: type 642, monocoque in composite carbon-fibre and Kevlar honeycomb. Brakes: ventilated outboard carbon-fibre discs, Brembo one piece 4-pot callipers. Length 4,400mm; width 2,130mm; height 1,004mm; kerb weight (with water and oil) 505kg

Prost and Alesi, fifth and third at the Monaco Grand Prix

1992

Constructors' Championship: 4th
Drivers: Jean Alesi (7th), Ivan Capelli (12th), Nicola Larini.
GP won: 0
F92-A
Engine: type E1 A-92, rear-mounted 65° V12. Transmission: rear-wheel drive, longitudinal semi-automatic 6-speed gearbox + reverse with electronic management, limited-slip differential. Chassis: composite carbon-fibre honeycomb. Brakes: ventilated carbon-fibre discs. Length 4,350mm; width 2,135mm; height 978mm; kerb weight (with water and oil) 505kg

Capelli at the Monaco Grand Prix

1993

Constructors' Championship: 4th
Drivers: Jean Alesi (6th), Gerhard Berger (8th).
GP won: 0
F93A
Engine: Ferrari 3500 (E2 A-93), rear-mounted 65° V12. Transmission: rear-wheel drive, semi-automatic, transverse 6-speed gearbox + reverse with electronic management, limited-slip differential. Chassis: composite carbon-fibre honeycomb. Brakes: ventilated carbon-fibre discs on all four wheels. Length 4,350mm; width 1,995mm; height 995mm; kerb weight (with water and oil) 505kg

Alesi, second, on his lap of honour at the Italian Grand Prix, Monza

1994

Constructors' Championship: 3rd
Drivers: Gerhard Berger (3rd), Jean Alesi
(5th), Nicola Larini (14th).
GP won: 1 — Germany 31 July
412 T1
Engine: Ferrari 3500 (F4 A-94), rear-
mounted 65° V12. Transmission: rear-
wheel drive, transverse semi-automatic
sequential 6-speed gearbox + reverse
with electronic control, limited-slip
differential. Chassis: composite
honeycomb with carbon-fibre. Brakes:
ventilated carbon-fibre discs. Length
4,495.5mm; width 1,995mm; height
995mm; kerb weight (with water and
oil) 505kg

Alesi and Todt

1995

Constructors' Championship: 3rd
Drivers: Jean Alesi (5th), Gerhard
Berger (6th).
GP won: 1 — Canada 11 June
412 T2
Engine: Ferrari 3000 (044/1), rear-
mounted 75° V12. Transmission: rear-
wheel drive, transverse semi-automatic
sequential 6-speed gearbox + reverse
with electronic control, limited-slip
differential. Chassis: tubular. Brakes:
ventilated carbon-fibre discs Length
4,380mm; width 1,995mm; height 980mm;
kerb weight (with water and oil) 595kg

*Alesi hitches a ride on Michael
Schumacher's Benetton*

1996

Constructors' Championship: 2nd
Drivers: Michael Schumacher (3rd), Eddie
Irvine (10th).
GP won: 3 — Spain 2 June, Belgium 25
August, Italy 8 September
F310
Engine: 3000 Ferrari (046), rear-mounted
75° V10. Transmission: rear-wheel drive,
semi-automatic sequential electronically
controlled transverse 6-speed gearbox +
reverse, limited-slip differential. Chassis:
carbon-fibre and composite honeycomb.
Brakes: ventilated carbon-fibre discs.
Length 4,355mm; width 1,995mm; height
970mm; kerb weight (with water and oil)
600kg (including driver)

*Schumacher celebrates his victory at the
Italian Grand Prix*

1997

Constructors' Championship: 2nd
Drivers: Eddie Irvine (7th), Michael
Schumacher (excluded).
GP won: 5 — Monaco 11 May, Canada 15
June, France 29 June, Belgium 24
August, Japan 12 October
F310 B
Engine: 3000 Ferrari (046/1B and
046/2), rear-mounted 75° V10.
Transmission: rear-wheel drive, transverse
semi-automatic sequential electronically
controlled 7-speed gearbox + reverse,
limited-slip differential. Chassis: carbon-
fibre and composite honeycomb. Brakes:
ventilated carbon-fibre discs. Length
4,358mm; width 1,995mm; height 970mm;
kerb weight (with water and oil) 600kg
(including driver)

*Schumacher wins the Japanese
Grand Prix*

1998

Constructors' Championship: 2nd
Drivers: Michael Schumacher (2nd), Eddie
Irvine (4th).
GP won: 6 — Argentina 12 April, Canada 7
June, France 28 June, Great Britain 12
July, Hungary 16 August, Italy 13
September
F300
Engine: Ferrari 047, rear-mounted 80°
V10. Transmission: rear-wheel drive,
longitudinal semi-automatic sequential
electronically controlled 7-speed gearbox
+ reverse, limited-slip differential. Chassis:
carbon-fibre and composite honeycomb.
Brakes: ventilated carbon-fibre discs.
Length 4,340mm; width 1,795mm; height
961mm; kerb weight (with water and oil)
600kg (including driver)

*Schumacher winning the Argentinian
Grand Prix*

1999

Constructors' Championship: 1st
Drivers: Eddie Irvine (2nd), Michael
Schumacher (5th), Mika Salo (10th).
GP won: 6 — Australia 7 March, San
Marino 2 May, Monaco 16 May, Austria
25 July, Germany 1 August, Malaysia
17 October
F399
Engine: 3000 Ferrari (048), rear-mounted
80° V10. Transmission: rear-wheel drive,
longitudinal semi-automatic sequential
electronically controlled 7-speed gearbox
+ reverse limited-slip differential. Chassis:
carbon-fibre and composite honeycomb.
Brakes: ventilated carbon-fibre discs.
Length 4,387mm; width 1,795mm; height
961mm; kerb weight (with water and oil)
600kg (including driver)

*Irvine mobbed by the press after his first
grand prix victory (Australia)*

2000

Constructors' Championship: 1st
Drivers: Michael Schumacher (1st),
Rubens Barrichello (4th).
GP won: 10 — Australia 12 March, Brazil
26 March, San Marino 9 April, Europe 21
May, Canada 18 June, Germany 30 July,
Italy 10 September, USA 24 September,
Japan 8 October, Malaysia 22 October
F1-2000
Engine: 3000 Ferrari (type 049), rear-
mounted 90° V10, dye-cast aluminium.
Transmission: rear-wheel drive, longitudinal
semi-automatic sequential electronically
controlled 7-speed gearbox + reverse,
limited-slip differential. Chassis: carbon-
fibre and composite honeycomb. Brakes:
ventilated carbon-fibre discs. Length
4,397mm; width 1,795mm; height 959mm;
kerb weight (with water and oil) 600kg
(including driver)

*Schumacher and the team celebrate
winning the drivers' championship*

2001

Constructors' Championship: 1st
Drivers: Michael Schumacher (1st),
Rubens Barrichello (3rd).
GP won: 9 — Australia 4 March, Malaysia
18 March, Spain 29 April, Monaco 27 May,
Europe 24 June, France 1 July, Hungary
19 August, Belgium 2 September, Japan
14 October
F2001
Engine: 3000 Ferrari (type 050), rear-
mounted 90° V10. Transmission: rear-
wheel drive, longitudinal semi-automatic
sequential electronically controlled
7-speed gearbox + reverse, limited-slip
differential. Chassis: carbon-fibre and
composite honeycomb. Brakes: on all four
discs. Length 4,445mm; width 1,796mm;
height 959mm; kerb weight (with water
and oil) 600kg (including driver)

Barrichello at the Japanese Grand Prix

2002

Constructors' Championship: 1st
Drivers: Michael Schumacher (1st), Rubens Barrichello (2nd).
GP won: 15 — Australia 3 March, Brazil 31 March, San Marino 14 April, Spain 28 April, Austria 12 May, Canada 9 June, Europe 23 June, Great Britain 7 July, France 21 July, Germany 28 July, Hungary 18 August, Belgium 1 September, Italy 15 September, USA 29 September, Japan 13 October
F2002
Engine: 3000 Ferrari (type 051), rear-mounted 90° V10. Transmission: semi-automatic sequential electronically controlled 7-speed gearbox + reverse, limited-slip differential. Chassis: carbon-fibre and honeycomb composite. Brakes: ventilated carbon-fibre disc brakes. Length 4,495mm; width 1,796mm; height 959mm; kerb weight (with water and oil) 600kg (including driver)

Schumacher celebrates winning the Australian Grand Prix

2003

Constructors' Championship: 1st
Drivers: Michael Schumacher (1st), Rubens Barrichello (4th).
GP won: 8 — San Marino 20 April, Spain 4 May, Austria 18 May, Canada 15 June, Great Britain 20 July, Italy 14 September, USA 28 September, Japan 12 October
F 2003-GA
Engine: 3000 Ferrari (type 052), rear-mounted 90° V10. Transmission: semi-automatic sequential electronically controlled 7-speed gearbox + reverse, limited-slip differential. Chassis: carbon-fibre and honeycomb composite. Brakes: ventilated carbon-fibre disc brakes. Length 4,545mm; width 1,796mm; height 959mm; kerb weight (with water and oil) 600kg (including driver)

Barrichello wins the Japanese Grand Prix

THE F2004 IN TESTING BEFORE THE BEGINNING OF THE NEW SEASON

Ferrari wishes to thank all those who through their effort, passion, dedication and determination, worked with modesty and pride to contribute to the achievements recorded in this book. They are the real secret of 'Formula Ferrari' Furthermore, we thank all our fans for their continued and warm support, which was never lacking, even during the most difficult moments.

Umberto Zapelloni would like to thank Ferrari who opened doors to some of its secret places for me, to the engineers and mechanics who answered my questions, to Luca Colajanni and Jean Todt who effectively edited the book. And naturally, thanks to Cristina and Federico who indulged me as I worked my way through to the end of this adventure.

Lucas Albers would like to thank Frank Luchetta, Robi Aebli, Bruno Macor Sabine Kehm, Ronni Ochsner, Marco Shelly and Willi Weber.